1944
THE ALLIES TRIUMPH

1944
THE ALLIES TRIUMPH

JOHN WESTWOOD

Grange
BOOKS

Published by Grange Books
An Imprint of Grange Books plc
The Grange
Grange Yard
London SE1 3AG

This edition published 1994

ISBN 1-85627-561-2

Produced by
Bison Books Ltd
Kimbolton House
117A Fulham Road
London SW3 6RL

Printed in Slovenia

Page 1: One month before D-Day, General
Montgomery receives Prime Minister Winston
Churchill as he pays a visit to the invasion troops
stationed in southeast England.

Pages 2-3: Mustang fighters in flight. The aircraft was
the best long-range Allied fighter of the war.

These pages: US landing craft off the Normandy
beaches on D-Day, note the small but ever-useful
LCVPs in the foreground.

CONTENTS

INTRODUCTION

Left: The long-range 5.5-inch howitzer, one of the mainstays of British artillery in World War II. This picture was taken during the Italian campaign.

Above: A meeting of the highest Anglo-American military planning body, the Joint Chiefs of Staff.

At the start of 1944 neither the Allies nor the remaining Axis powers were quite sure where they were going. In the case of Germany and Japan this was not surprising, for they had not prepared for a situation in which their armies were no longer victorious. For the USA and Britain the goal was clear, and 1943 had seen some steps toward it, but victory did not seem absolutely certain because that year had also witnessed several reverses.

The bomber offensive, long seen as the only way to get at Germany short of launching a second front, was not going as well as had been hoped or claimed. The Italian campaign had sunk into stalemate. In early 1943 the U-boats had been triumphant in the North Atlantic and, although they had been mastered in the nick of time, just one unexpected technical breakthrough might restore them to their status as the most dangerous enemy. The USA had turned the tide in the Pacific but enough casualties had been in-curred, and enough naval encounters had been unsuccessful, to suggest that victory here would not be easy. And public opinion, which was both the strength and weakness of democracies at war, was showing signs of weariness. Only Stalin's Russia seemed to know where it was going, but in Stalin's Russia doubt was a capital offense.

1942 had clearly been the year in which the Axis powers had been stopped in their tracks, and in retrospect 1943 can be seen as the year of the turnround, but at the start of 1944 this seemed less certain. There was still a fear that something unexpected, or a sudden technological leap by one of the Axis powers, might yet confront the Allies with another succession of reverses like those of early 1942. A decision had been made that Germany would be defeated in the West by a land campaign beginning on the Normandy beaches, but the success of such a landing was far from guaranteed. As for Japan, its domination by a clique of super-militarists seemed to ensure

Below: At the Quebec Conference of 1943, the Canadian Prime Minister Mackenzie King (center), President Roosevelt and Churchill take time off to meet the press.

that bitter fighting would continue long after its position had become hopeless.

Now, half a century or so later, 1943 can also be seen to divide the early war from the late war, giving a preview of how power and influence would be distributed at war's end. In particular, the USA had emerged as a superpower; one fact emphasizing her dominance was that in 1943 she was conducting the campaign against Japan while devoting four-fifths of her effort to the war in Europe. No other country could fight two great campaigns so successfully at the same time. Germany had tried but was failing, while Britain in 1942 had been endeavoring to fight on three fronts and as a result had been humiliated in the Far East. Russia had carefully abstained from fighting Japan so long as Germany was still active, but at the Tehran Conference in late 1943 the USSR did seem to emerge as another superpower.

Britain, which had been engaged since 1939 and which for a year had fought alone, did

Above: German walking wounded retire from the field in the preliminary fighting around Stalingrad, the battle that changed the course of the war on the Eastern Front.

Left: A more comfortable evacuation. Allied soldiers wounded in the Sicily campaign leave Syracuse by hospital ship probably heading for North Africa.

ARCTIC OCEAN

Barents Sea

LIBERATED BY ALLIES
19 NOVEMBER 1942 – 4 JULY 1943
4 JULY 1943 – 23 JUNE 1944

ALLIED FRONT LINES
— — — 2 FEBRUARY 1943
— · — · — 4 JULY 1943
— ·· — ·· — 14 JANUARY 1944
— — — — 23 JUNE 1944

MILES
0   500
KILOMETERS
0   800

REYKJAVIK
ICELAND

PETSAMO
MURMANSK
NARVIK
White Sea
ARCHANGEL

TRONDHEIM
FINLAND
PETROZAVODSK

VIIPURI
L. Ladoga
Jan 1943
Leningrad relieved

BERGEN
HELSINKI
LENINGRAD

OSLO
STOCKHOLM
TALLINN

RIGA
PSKOV
MOSCOW
R U S S I A
TULA

ATLANTIC

NORTH
SEA
EDINBURGH
GREAT
DENMARK COPENHAGEN
KAUNAS
SMOLENSK
VORONEZH
KURSK

OCEAN
EIRE
DUBLIN
LIVERPOOL
BRITAIN
KÖNIGSBERG
E. PRUSSIA
MINSK
Vistula
4–23 July 1943
Battle of Kursk
KHARKOV
STALINGRAD

NETH.
HAMBURG
DANZIG
Caspian
Sea

6 June 1944
D-day: Allied forces
land in Normandy
AMSTERDAM
BERLIN
WARSAW
POLAND
KIEV
Dnieper
ZAPOROZHYE
Don
ROSTOV

LONDON
COLOGNE
GERMANY
GROZNY

CHERBOURG
BRUSSELS
BELG.
PRAGUE
LVOV
ODESSA
NOVOROSSIISK

CAEN
LUX.
SLOVAKIA
SEVASTOPOL
TIFLIS

PARIS
Danube
MUNICH VIENNA
HUNGARY
BLACK SEA

FRANCE
BERNE
SWITZ.
BUDAPEST

VICHY
MILAN
RUMANIA
BUCHAREST

Bay of
Biscay
TURIN
VENICE

BORDEAUX
MARSEILLES
FLORENCE
BELGRADE
YUGOSLAVIA
Danube
BULGARIA
SOFIA
ANKARA
IRAN

27 Jan–18 May 1944
Battles for Cassino
ISTANBUL
T U R K E Y

LISBON
MADRID
15 Aug 1944
Landings in
St Tropez area
Corsica
ROME
CASSINO
ALBANIA

SPAIN
22 Jan 1944
Landings at Anzio
ANZIO
NAPLES
SALERNO
8 Sept 1943
Italy surrenders
GREECE

PORTUGAL
Sept 1943
Landings at Reggio (3rd)
and Salerno (9th)
PALERMO
REGGIO
ATHENS
Dodecanese
SYRIA
(Free Fr)
IRAQ
(Br)

GIBRALTAR (Br)
SP. MOR.
Sicily
Cyprus
(Br)
DAMASCUS

CASABLANCA
ORAN
ALGIERS
BÔNE
TUNIS
C. Bon
10 July 1943
Allied forces
land in Sicily
Crete

ALGERIA
(Free French)
KASSERINE
MALTA
PALESTINE
(Br)
JERUSALEM
AMMAN
TRANSJORDAN
(Br)

MOROCCO
(Fr)
TUNISIA
(Free Fr)
MARETH
11 May 1943
Axis forces in N.
Africa surrender
TOBRUK
ALEXANDRIA

TRIPOLI
SIRTE
EL AGHEILA
L I B Y A
BENGHAZI
EL ALAMEIN
Nile
Suez
Canal
CAIRO
SAUDI
ARABIA
EGYPT
(Br prot.)

Above: The ebb and flow of World War II in Europe, 1942-44. In the east and south, German-occupied territory had been contracting for 18 months before D-Day began the Allied offensive from the west.

not have the strength to fight simultaneously in the East and in Europe. Lend-Lease gave her the weapons she needed at no cost, but the terms of the deal guaranteed that she would lack foreign currency reserves. By late 1943 she had also come to the end of her man-power resources. Unlike Germany, where the Nazi regime held to the view that even in wartime a woman's place was the kitchen, Britain had used all her reserve of female labor, which had gone mainly to replace workers called up for service. This had not been enough, and munitions output had to fall in 1944 simply because Britain lacked the resources to keep pace.

In 1942 British munitions production had exceeded American, but by the end of 1943 the USA was producing four times as much as Britain. A final scrape of the barrel had come in late 1943, when British males began to be drafted to work as coal miners. This was at a time when the mines were threatened by strikes; war-weariness and no sight of im-mediate victory had its effect from mid-1943 in Britain, with industrial strikes constantly threatened and occasionally enacted. It would not be until the invasion of Normandy in 1944 that British workers would regain something of their previous war-winning spirit.

Above: Sicilians contemplate the cost of war after the Allied invasion.

Below: At the beginning of 1944 Hitler was already suffering from stress and over-medication, although he seemed robust enough in public.

For two other main players of the early war, 1943 witnessed a radical change of course. Fascist Italy, which had taken the opportunity of France's imminent defeat in 1940 to join in the war, ceased to be fascist Italy as soon as the Allies landed in Sicily. In September 1943, when the Allies invaded Italy proper, the new Italian regime decided that the moment for surrender had arrived, and henceforth the Axis campaign in Italy was fought by the Germans alone. Meanwhile, France was re-emerging as a power. Although France itself was still run by the Germans and the Vichy French regime, in the French Empire more and more individuals

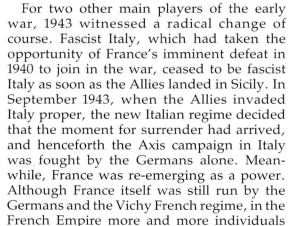

Above: Admiral Dönitz (center) supervises the U-boat campaign from his Berlin headquarters. He was later to be Hitler's successor.

Above: Charles de Gaulle, as he was during World War II, when his resolution and intelligence gave the Free French great influence in the conduct of the war. He combined intense patriotism with an intellectual approach to the conduct of war.

and units had decided to follow the example of those who had rallied to de Gaulle's Free French in 1940. The main source of manpower lay in French North Africa, where the Allies had expelled the Italians and Germans in early 1943. French and French colonial forces henceforth made a useful contribution to the Allied strength.

German power had always resided in its army and its air force, and both were in a worse state than either they or their enemies realized in 1943. The German defeat of Stalingrad early that year and the Russian offensives which followed were more than a material and psychological setback; they marked the point when German losses were so great that a full recovery was never made. German industry did wonders in replacing the lost aircraft, and tanks and guns, but hardened, experienced men had been lost for ever. New recruits were still good, but not quite as good as their predecessors, largely because it was impossible to give them all the training they needed. The new tanks were far better than those they replaced, but the same could not be said for the new aircraft, even though before the war was finished a few German jet planes would see active service.

Germany's problem was not merely that she had met defeat in Russia and North Africa, but that she had no clear-cut, thought-out policies for the circumstances that developed in 1943. While her opening campaigns in 1940 and 1941 had been planned meticulously and executed boldly, little thought had been given to the possibility that the offensive in Russia might run out of steam. Nor had the virtual "second-front situation" in Italy been anticipated when, in 1941, the first German troops had been sent to lend a hand to Mussolini in Libya.

On the Eastern Front the German army was losing the initiative as it reacted to one crisis after another, with Hitler overruling his generals on some crucial issues. Repeatedly, the German forces held on too long in hopeless situations during the succession of Soviet offensives that followed Stalingrad. Hitler discouraged retreats, so troops that might have been extricated in time to create new defense lines were badly mauled by the advancing Russians. The Russian offensive, backed by seemingly unlimited manpower, managed in the course of 1943 to recapture Kiev and Smolensk and partly lift the 16-month siege of Leningrad. But, despite these defeats, the German army in Russia in late 1943 presented an appearance of potential strength, waiting its moment for a counter-offensive.

As 1944 would show, the fear that the Axis powers might produce new war-winning weapons had some justification. Although the Nazi regime, on the advice of its nuclear scientists, gave the creation of an atomic bomb low priority, it was at the same time driving forward with new weapons that had a greater likelihood of getting into production before the war ended. Luckily for the Allies, each of these developments came into use just too late. Thus the acoustic torpedo, which for a few weeks seemed likely to restore U-boats to their old menacing status, came into production just after the Allies had found better ways of countering the submarine menace. Again, the V-1 flying bomb and the V-2 rocket would make life very uncomfortable for Britain in 1944, but the launching sites would be overrun by the Allies before too much damage had been done.

In some ways, 1943 was a year in which some long-standing accounts had been closed. The end of Italian fascism was one such ending. The demise of German sea power was another. At the very end of 1943 the last serviceable German battleship, *Scharnhorst*, was sent to the bottom after a

Right: The primitive but alarming German V-1 missile, or "Doodlebug." This example was photographed immediately after its launch.

Below: Forerunner of the modern ballistic missile, the German V-2 brought alarm to southeast England from 1944 onward, though damage was relatively light.

gun engagement with British ships covering a convoy to Russia. As the German admiral and his staff were killed, the apparently inept handling of the German battleship has never been explained. Certainly its movements invited destruction, and the suspicion must remain that the German navy was not only short of surface ships but also of staff officers capable of handling them. A bigger German battleship lurking in Norwegian fjords and presenting a threat to Russian convoys was *Tirpitz*, but attacks by midget submarines put her out of action in 1943, ready for her final destruction by bombing in 1944.

The other, more lethal, branch of the German navy also had a bad year in 1943. It would never regain the initiative, but the Allies could not know this. At first things had gone well for the U-boats. New "wolf-pack" tactics in which the submarines conducted their business mainly in groups on the surface, wreaked havoc among Atlantic convoys, and the U-boats were also spreading their field of activity to the south Atlantic and Indian Ocean. March 1943 was the worst month for Allied shipping, with 477,000 tons falling victim to submarines and only 12 U-boats sunk. Shortage of escorts and the reluctance of both the US and British air forces to divert bombers to maritime work was the main Allied weakness, but after spring 1943 these faults were remedied. More bombers were diverted and the US Navy made available scores of extra escorts. Portugal, at last concluding that Germany would probably not win the war, made airbases available in the Azores.

This, and the introduction of escort carriers – simple aircraft carriers produced by putting flight decks on merchant ship hulls – eliminated the mid-Atlantic gap which previously had been out of range of Allied aircraft. In the last three months of 1943 only 146,000 tons of shipping were lost and over those three months 53 U-boats had been sunk. Especially successful in the far reaches of the central Atlantic were US Navy task groups composed specially for submarine hunting. They consisted of an escort carrier armed with Wildcat fighters and Avengers, the latter capable of dropping bombs, torpedoes and depth-charges, with an escort of whatever old destroyers might be available.

But the majority of U-boat losses were incurred by air attack close to the submarines' Biscay bases. For a time the U-boat command tried to remedy this vulnerability by strengthening the anti-aircraft defense of submarines so that instead of diving on sight of enemy aircraft they could beat them off. At the same time a big effort was made to develop and fit search receivers that could detect Allied aircraft radar beams, thereby giving advance warning that a U-boat had been targeted. Neither of these measures

solved the problem and the U-boat service, while continuing to send submarines out into the Atlantic, where they had a poor chance of success and survival, waited patiently for new technology. New propulsion methods, giving high underwater speeds, were producing encouraging results, but production submarines with this hydrogen peroxide system of propulsion appeared only at the very end of the war.

The *schnorkel*, reducing submarine vulnerability by permitting battery recharging while under water, was at an advanced stage at the end of 1943 and was expected to bring great gains in 1944, but in the event arrived too late. The acoustic torpedo, homing on to the propellers of target ships, began in late 1943 with a burst of success when several escorts of a transatlantic convoy were sunk, but the Allies soon devised countermeasures. Had the war continued into 1946 the U-boat might possibly have made a come-back, but it would really have needed more air support. 1943 was already showing that the German air force was as reluctant as the British to divert effort to the Atlantic. Just as the British suffered grievously after Bomber Command declined to attack the bomb-proof concrete pens of U-boats in French Atlantic ports while they were in course of construction – and still vulnerable – so did the U-boat service suffer when the Luftwaffe declined to help with the problem of Allied air attacks on U-boats in the Bay of Biscay.

Thus by the end of 1943, with the departure from the scene of German and Italian battle-fleets, the British navy no longer had to face the impossible task of a war on three oceans. Big ships could be released for the Pacific, but several US admirals were against such a transfer. Although this was explained at the time as a reaction to the difficulties that a British Pacific squadron would impose, because it would not fit into the US task-force system of fleet management, the real reason was probably inter-navy jealousy. The US Navy, having successfully weathered the Japanese storm and regained the initiative, did not wish to share victory with another naval power. For the time being, therefore, British naval participation was restricted to the Indian Ocean, although in 1945, prompted by President Roosevelt, the US Chiefs of Staff would accept a British contribution to the Pacific war.

This kind of jealousy, which could take the form of inter-service or inter-nation tension, was found in both the Allied and Axis camps, but the Allies coped with it much more successfully than did their enemies. Anglo-

American rivalry was remarkably muted in the circumstances: the British had regarded themselves as senior combatants, having weathered 1940 alone, but soon saw that the USA, with its huge resources, would inevitably dominate the Allied side. But the British also saw that this US domination was a necessary price of victory over the Axis powers and therefore accepted it. Churchill put up a strong rearguard action aimed at preserving British influence, but well knew that the US government did not approve of the British Empire and that at the end of the war Britain would be impoverished and dependent on US goodwill and help.

In 1943 General Dwight Eisenhower was rising fast in the Allied command and this was a man with the tact and modesty needed to smooth over the inevitable tensions that would occur as British and Americans fought side by side. He was not helped by some of the US generals. Both Clark and Patton, gifted soldiers, were afflicted with oversensitivity to image. For them the glory of the army, the USA, and themselves sometimes seemed to outweigh all other considerations, although Patton, unlike Clark, did not deliberately disobey the instructions of a commanding British general. British generals were less worried about image and reputation, although the one big exception, Montgomery, could not fail to raise the hackles of US colleagues. Even the patient Eisenhower was finding him hard to bear.

Most Anglo-American differences, however, were honest differences of opinion, and these were thrashed out by the Combined Chiefs of Staff, who sometimes conferred with the president and prime minister at meetings in different parts of the world. The fundamental difference, which had become apparent during 1942, was that Britain and the USA had different philosophies of conducting a war. Britain, with her limited resources, and psychologically conditioned by memory of the slaughter of World War I, preferred a strategy that would incur the fewest losses, even if such a strategy took more time.

The Americans, on the other hand, were more in favor of exploiting their preponderance of men and material with direct highpower assaults on the enemy's strongpoints. Britain, and Churchill in particular, sought to postpone the landings in northern France and to advance on Germany from completely different, less defended, directions, whereas the US (and Russia) felt such landings were the quickest way to get to grips with German power. However, in 1943 an invasion of northern France in summer 1944 had been finally accepted by the British.

Not only were there inter-Allied differences, but also inter-service rivalries. Although there were good reasons for the US decision to regard the war in Europe as the first priority, leaving a final quelling of Japan until later, there were nevertheless sound arguments for putting Japan first and Hitler second. Possibly, if Hitler in 1941 had not made the gross strategic error of declaring war on the US after Pearl Harbor, this order of priorities might have been different. But certainly a factor in the Europe-first decision was the US Army's desire to play a leading role. In the Pacific war it could only play second fiddle to the US Navy.

Both the USA and Britain suffered from inter-service and inter-arm rivalries centering over the role of strategic bombing. The US Air Force's main advocate of the primacy of bombing was its chief, Henry H. Arnold, a strong, forthright man. Even more strong and forthright was Air Marshal Arthur Harris, who became head of British Bomber Command. This was a man who believed totally in the ability of heavy bombing, alone, to put Germany out of the war. Knowing that his bombers could not drop their bombs with any precision, nor indeed navigate with any certainty, he advocated what was euphemistically termed area bombing. Having seen, between the wars, how RAF bombers sowed terror in the hearts of dissident Middle Eastern tribesmen, Harris believed that the same effect could be achieved with the Germans.

Immense industrial resources and highclass manpower were devoted to building up Bomber Command for its mission, adopted in 1942, of obliterating German civilians. Cities with large areas of wooden housing were favored, but although Germans were killed in large numbers, the effect on morale seems to have been minimal. And not only did Bomber Command represent a voracious consumer of resources, it was also reluctant to give help to the British army and navy. In particular, it only grudgingly made aircraft available for the Battle of the Atlantic, even when Britain faced catastrophe in the worst days of the U-boat campaign. Characteristically, its preferred mode of attack against the U-boat danger was the bombing of U-boat pens in French ports, even though its bombs could not penetrate them.

Arnold also had great faith in the bomber.

Far left: The German *U-101*, one of the VII-b type submarines whose construction started just before the war.

Below, far left: An Allied tanker falls victim to a U-boat in the Battle of the Atlantic.

Below: General Eisenhower, the Allied supreme commander, photographed in late 1944 when he was visiting a US division fighting in Belgium.

Above: The USS *Tinosa*, one of the war-built "Gato" class submarines, returns from one of her several successful patrols. Completed in 1943, she and her sisters throttled Japanese shipping routes in 1944 and 1945.

Above, far right: US Marines on Tarawa (November 1943) make the perilous dash from the beachhead into the interior of the island.

Far right: Two Marines searching for the Japanese defenders of Bougainville Island. At this stage of the operation, snipers were the main danger.

American bomb-aiming was less inaccurate, so Arnold rejected the area bombing concept in favor of what was rather flatteringly called precision bombing. The situation arose that the RAF conducted it anti-population raids during the night and the US Air Force its precision bombing by day. In 1943 neither was having much success, although both made great claims, and until the planning of the Normandy invasion concentrated minds on realities the school of thought that considered that the bomber, alone, could win the war, was predominant. But planning for the invasion made clear that the bomber would merely be an important adjunct for victory, and that victory would be sealed by the occupation of Germany by the Allied armies, not their air forces.

So, much to their disgust, the heads of the US and British bomber services were subordinated to the supreme command, and found that their long-cherished ambition to win the war by reducing Germany to ashes was no longer on the agenda. Instead, bombers were to be directed to targets of direct relevance to the Normandy invasion and they would do well in this role, partly because they were thereby used for a purpose to which they were very suited.

The failure of the politicians to quell the demands of their bomber services until late 1943 was the worst instance of lack of inter-service cooperation on the Allied side. After the war Harris and Arnold were heavily criticized, but really the successive bombing policies had been political decisions. Harris and Arnold had merely advocated what they believed to be the best course. Elsewhere on the Allied side inter-service cooperation was good. In the Libyan campaign the British had worked out a system whereby mobile radio centers accompanied troop formations into action, and swiftly called for air support from planes waiting in the air. This technique was repeated in subsequent campaigns, and was highly successful.

In Germany inter-service cooperation was often lacking. Hitler had the power to impose such cooperation, but often he did not do so, and when he did his instructions were not always followed. In any case his demands were not always well-advised, and the long-standing impression that Hitler's interventions in strategy and tactics were usually unhelpful is supported by modern research. Hitler had little understanding of the principles of air warfare, and could not grasp that aircraft might need to be kept in reserve.

The German navy was by far the junior service and was often openly despised. This meant that its advice, even in matters close to its expertise, was ignored and often not even invited. Meanwhile the army continued to be the most prestigious service, and regarded the air force with suspicion. Suspicion gradually turned to open contempt as the war progressed, with the Luftwaffe failing to give the army the support it needed. Although army support was regarded as the first role of the Luftwaffe, Allied pressure from 1943 onward meant that fighter production had priority. In battle areas, local Luftwaffe ground-support squadrons were under the authority of the local ground commander, so it was impossible to apply a centralized control, with squadrons shifted from sector to sector in accordance with need.

On the whole, the Luftwaffe was in a bad state by the end of 1943. Allied planners, unlike German, had realized that the only way to secure command of the air was to conduct the air war not as a succession of battles, but as a continuous, daily pressure in which German aircraft would be inexorably destroyed until destruction rates exceeded production rates. Secure in the knowledge that the US had big reserves both of aircraft production

and aircrew, the Allies could afford this long battle of attrition. By 1944 not only were the Germans outnumbered, but the percentage of their aircraft awaiting repair was very high; this in turn meant that an increasing proportion were destroyed on the ground.

Japan showed the Axis powers at their worst, both in terms of inter-ally and inter-service relations. Japan had disappointed Hitler by not declaring war on Soviet Russia at the time of the German invasion but, nevertheless, Hitler had declared war on the US in support of Japan, even though that was against his strategic interest. But there was very little military support or cooperation, even though Japan would have benefited enormously from German assistance in tank and aircraft design. Some German U-boats did operate from a base in Japan-held Malaya, but this was a small affair.

Axis talk of their "Tripartite cooperation" in fact was little more than that. Tokyo hesitated to share its thoughts with Italy, believing that Italians could not be trusted with secrets. Italy's surrender seemed to confirm the Japanese belief that Italy was a fairly useless ally. But by that time Tokyo had begun to doubt the use of its German alliance as well. In March 1943 it actually sent a mission to Germany entrusted with finding out what Germany's position really was like. The mission's reports were pessimistic. Germany was very unlikely to win the war, it said, because not only was the Eastern Front situation dangerous, but Germany had severe problems of supply and production.

In 1943 the Japanese navy and army were still in a state of acute rivalry, if not hostility, and the army's dominance of the cabinet in Tokyo meant that in big issues the navy

Below: An everyday scene in the Guadalcanal operations as Marines set out on a mission behind Japanese lines. The battle lasted six months and gave the US forces a jumping-off point for other advances in the Solomon Islands.

would not win the argument. Both services, like the American, ran their own air forces, but the Japanese navy's air force was stronger than the army's. There was no cooperation and each service ordered its own designs of aircraft. Even the ammunition for the guns of army and navy aircraft was not interchangeable. When the Americans invaded Guadalcanal the Japanese army did not know that the navy had built airfields there. When radar stations were installed to cover Japan, both services insisted on having their own, so army and navy stations were built almost side-by-side, a duplication of effort that Japan could not afford.

Like Germany, Japan had no clear idea of what to do next, once the early victories had come to an end. Conflict between the army and navy, and between the army high command and the war ministry, made it difficult either to reach agreements or to carry them out. When the Americans attacked Guadalcanal, the war ministry, on grounds of shipping shortage, refused to agree with the army command's demand that Guadalcanal should not be abandoned. On this, as on a few other occasions, army and ministry staff actually came to blows.

The planners eventually fixed on an outer defense perimeter that had to be held at all costs. This encompassed most of the Japanese conquests and was to bar the Americans from territories from where they could fly bombers over Japan itself. The aim, in which wishful thinking played as great a role as in previous Japanese strategic concepts, was to defend this line until such time as the Allied powers decided to make peace, from boredom if not from military defeat. But already in 1943 the Americans and Australians were threatening that outer perimeter. In New Guinea, after fighting hard rearguard actions, they were about to launch counter-offensives, while in the Pacific the Americans had landed in the Solomon Islands and were intent on proceeding northward, island by island. Their tactics were far from perfect, and neither was their equipment, but they were showing that the Japanese could at least be thrown back, and at the same time amassing painful experience that would benefit later operations as the ring closed about Japan.

The speed of the turnround in Japan's fortunes is exemplified by the Solomon Islands. The Japanese landed here in January 1942, but in August the US forces began their campaign to win them back. Between these two events the Japanese navy had been routed at Midway and lost the best part of its air

strength. In February 1943, after months of bitter fighting on various islands, the key island of Guadalcanal was finally captured by the Americans.

Further islands in this chain remained to be captured, but the US command was introducing the strategy of leap-frogging, in which just a few islands were captured and the remainder left to wither on the vine. By late 1943 the Americans had a foothold in Bougainville, although the Japanese com-

Above: An incident in the Bougainville campaign. A US light tank has been crippled by a land mine and its commander (his body just visible at the rear of the tank) killed by Japanese rifle fire.

Above right: Australian infantrymen moving up to attack the last Japanese strongpoint in Papua. By this time, the Japanese were exhausted and could offer little resistance.

mand was determined to eject them. Here, as elsewhere, much depended on sea power as the Japanese endeavored to slip reinforcements into contested islands. Many small naval engagements took place, mainly at night because that was when conditions were most favorable for the Japanese penetration. Not all these engagements were won by the Americans, but with its fewer resources the Japanese navy suffered considerably more than the American.

The Japanese high command was well aware by late 1943 that Japan had lost the war, but had no immediate intention of surrendering. Japan's Prime Minister and War Minister Tojo, shortly before his execution after the war, revealed that the command at this time saw three US initiatives for which it seemed impossible to find a remedy. One, unexpectedly, was the ability of US submarines to disrupt the essential supply route linking the southwestern Pacific and Japan. Whether this threat was as insuperable as the Japanese imagined is doubtful; to a large extent they were simply victims of their own ideology, being unwilling to adopt the convoy system or even to devote ships and aircraft to defensive tasks. The second Japanese anxiety revolved around the US fast carrier forces, which after Midway seemed unbeatable and capable of projecting force wherever the US command saw fit. Thirdly, there was the US technique of leap-frogging. This had not been anticipated by the Japanese and it was deadly, not so much because it won back territory for the Americans but because it condemned to irrelevance the substantial Japanese forces on the islands that had been leapfrogged.

NORMANDY

Previous pages:
Protected by barrage
balloons and the 20mm
guns of the USS *Ancon*
(the amphibious force
flagship on D-Day),
American infantry in LCIs
make the Channel
crossing to Normandy.

Below: General
Eisenhower leads a press
conference in early 1944.
On his right is Sir Arthur
Tedder, then Admiral
Bertram Ramsay and
General Omar Bradley.
General Bernard
Montgomery sits cagily
on Eisenhower's left.

Operation Overlord, the invasion of France across the English Channel, was the most critical operation of the entire war in Europe. Seaborne landings are so perilous, and the material and emotional capital placed in this enterprise was so great, that not only the day of the landing, D-Day (June 6), but the following days might well have witnessed a reversal of Allied fortunes that could have taken years to overcome.

Churchill, for one, had long sought to postpone this project; as in World War I, he was most interested in what he called "soft underbellies," but his American and Russian Allies were not sympathetic to his plea for landings in the Balkans, or in southern France, instead of the grand cross-Channel enterprise. For a time shortage of landing craft, partly a result of Churchill's preference

for building bombers, was a genuine reason to postpone D-Day, but eventually the British accepted May 1944 as the date of this operation. Later, the date was pushed back a month, but that was a mere detail in the intense planning and logistical movements that reached a climax during early 1944.

The British had a poor record in seaborne invasions. Many generals had personal "never again" memories of Gallipoli in 1915, and in earlier British wars there had been similar failures, one of which was celebrated in the satirical song about the Duke of York's men marching up, and then down, achieving nothing. Yet in the Crimean War the seaborne landings had proceeded quite smoothly, but cynics said that this was because the British were carefully watched by their French allies on that occasion. In 1944, of

course, they would be watched by their powerful Allies the Americans. As things turned out, the invasion was a great success and the British performed impeccably. Probably this was not because they were under US oversight but because the conditions of the invasion gave scope for work that the British did well: maritime action and organization, technical ingenuity, and deception. As for the Americans, they had already learned lessons from their Pacific operations, and were confident that their material superiority would win the day.

The most crucial issue facing the planners was choice of landing place; everything else depended on this. Disembarkation required firm beaches that were not overlooked by headlands from which enfilading fire could be brought down on the invaders at their most vulnerable stage. Gently sloping beaches, extensive enough to permit landings on a wide front, were ideal. Because supply would be such an enormous undertaking, the proximity of a good and easily captured port was all-important.

Behind the landing place, an important factor was absence of natural obstacles that might hamper extension of beachheads and

Above: Paratroop pathfinders, entrusted with lighting beacons to guide the main landing, synchronize their watches at the beginning of Operation Overlord.

Left: Royal Marines disembark, one disastrously, onto the Normandy beaches during D-Day. The men are on Juno Beach.

the eventual advance toward Paris and the Low Countries. A short sea crossing was an advantage, ensuring that troops would arrive fresh, and reducing the distance over which vessels would be vulnerable. A short sea crossing also implied a shorter distance from British airfields, which would enable land-based fighters to spend more time over the beaches.

Thanks largely to British staffwork, that for two years had been studying such an invasion, the different arms and the different countries had little difficulty in reaching agreement on the place of invasion; one possible source of discord was avoided by keeping de Gaulle's Free French officers out of the discussion. In the end, as usual, compromises had to be reached, and the Bay of the Seine in Normandy was chosen. This gave space for five separate landing areas, and the beaches met most requirements. However, a fairly long Channel crossing was involved and the troops, once landed, would have to force crossings of the Seine before moving east toward Belgium and Germany.

Seaborne invasions, though highly risky, do have some things in their favor, and this was especially true in 1944, when the Allies had command of the sea and of the air, and knew exactly where their blow would fall. Conversely, the Germans defending what was somewhat grandiosely called the Atlantic Wall, were handicapped by the need to defend a huge coastline, not knowing where the landings would be.

Weather and tides ensured that the Germans at certain periods could relax, knowing that invasion could not be on its way, but only good reconnaissance and intelligence could tell them where the blow would fall. Without such knowledge it was difficult to concentrate forces against the invaders at their weakest moment, the landings themselves. On the other hand, the alternative of keeping a large reserve inland and then sending it against the invaders would allow the latter time to build strong beachheads. The two German commanders, Rommel and Rundstedt, differed on this and in the end there was a kind of compromise between Rommel's advocacy of distributing defenses along the coast line and Rundstedt's preference for a central reserve. In fact, neither this compromise nor either of the two alternatives was satisfactory; the best hope of success for the Germans was bad luck or bad management on the Allied side, and although these were not entirely absent on D-Day, they were never serious enough to bring a major German victory.

Good intelligence of what was happening in southern England might have enabled the Germans to correctly predict the landing place. But Allied counter-intelligence and confidentiality were good, and without command of the air effective German reconnaissance was impossible. The British skilfully gave the impression that the landings would be farther east, in the Calais area. This was where most of the German command expected them in any case, since the shortest Channel crossing was here, the Seine no longer a barrier, and there were ports close by. The British, with some judicious troop movements and wooden construction work, presented a picture of immense troop and boat concentrations in southeast England,

Above: An LCVP (Landing Craft Vehicle Personnel) carries US infantrymen toward their landing point. They are destined for a very unpleasant day on Omaha Beach.

Right: The Canadian 3rd Infantry and 2nd Armored Brigades come ashore on D-Day at Juno Beach.

and the RAF ensured that a few German reconnaissance aircraft would find a gap in the air defenses precisely there. Other devices like intense radio activity were used to give the same impression.

The German army and navy had different opinions about where the landings would be. The army swallowed the British disinformation and thought the eastern end of the Channel, around the Somme estuary, would be the spot. Not only did it see the importance of the proximity of Paris and the Low Countries, and the avoidance of the Seine barrier, but it also argued that the launching sites for the V-1 flying bombs aimed at London were positioned in this area and for that reason, if no other, the Allies would be compelled to land there.

The navy, on the other hand, knowing how the area around the Somme estuary could be swept by unobstructed westerly winds, and seeing the irregular structure of the coast, thought the Allies would be unlikely to land there, and as the extreme west was too rocky, the central coast was left as the most likely choice. Along that central sector, the area known as the Bay of the Seine offered broad beaches, sheltered from the westerlies. Thus the navy was convinced that a landing would be in that area, and was right. However, the navy, being directly subordinated to the military command in this area, had little influence.

Nor could the navy get its way on the siting of coastal batteries. Hitler was inclined toward Rundstedt's view that the coast itself should be thinly defended, with all hopes placed on a mobile reserve. This meant that most of the guns defending the coast would also be inland and would therefore use indirect fire, controlled by forward observers. The navy saw that only direct, aimed, fire could deal with the fast-moving invasion craft, but its views were again little heeded.

A minefield had been laid covering the Bay of the Seine earlier in the war, but little of it was left in 1944. The German navy's attempt to re-lay it were unsuccessful because, having command both of the sea and the air, the Allies were able to devastate the minelayers. By that stage of the war the German naval command could deploy only a few dozen E-boats (motor torpedo boats) in the Channel, but because of superior Allied radar these were invariably spotted and attacked. There could be no question, therefore, of a constant sea patrol to gain early warning of an invasion fleet. The German air force was equally weak in this theater, so reliable air reconnaissance was also unavailable. Having

Above: Omaha Beach soon after the landings. The picture gives a good impression of the enormous number and variety of supporting ships. The beach has been cleared and supply vehicles are being landed.

Above, far right: A US beach battalion takes over German slit trenches some days after the invasion.

Far right: Part of the British 50th Infantry Division passes down a Normandy street a short distance from Gold Beach.

32 divisions poised to move where required, early warning would have been of immense help to the German command, especially as the Allies planned, for logistic reasons, to land only five divisions on D-Day, with six more to follow when space had been won for them on land.

Bad weather in the Channel forced the Supreme Allied Commander, Eisenhower, to postpone the operation. Then, a day late and with considerable misgiving, Eisenhower launched Operation Overlord. He was lucky, for the weather did improve. For the Germans, this sequence meant that the Allied invasion force appeared just when it was not expected, at a period of foul weather. Many German officers had taken advantage of the bad weather, and the consequent improbability of a landing, to enjoy recreations away from their units.

The operation began when US and British airborne forces, making use of gliders, landed and established themselves at the west and east ends of the invasion area. That was at 0200 hours on June 6. The beaches were then bombed, with a numerous collection of fairly aged warships adding their shellfire to the general devastation. It was during the naval bombardment that other Allied nations like France, Belgium and Holland were able to make a contribution. Among these the French had the most strength, being equipped with cruisers. One of the latter, *Georges Leygues*, (known to US seamen as "*George's Legs*") took the chance a few days after the bombardment to send a party ashore, where it was presented with a bill from the local village mayor for the destruction of 70 cows.

By this stage of the war it was recognized that neither bombers nor naval gunners could produce pinpoint accuracy, and to destroy guns emplaced in steel and concrete casemates only a direct hit was effective.

Research in 1943 had indicated that for a 90 percent chance of hitting all the guns of a four-gun battery 15,500 bombs needed to be dropped. Naval shellfire was also inaccurate, but less so: 500 heavy shells were needed for the same 90 percent chance. But the naval concentration of heavy guns and the cease-less assault of thousands of aircraft ensured the statistical probability that was needed. Moreover, whereas the difficult-to-obtain direct hit was required to destroy a gun, the more numerous near-misses could cause temporary cessation of fire by damaging in-struments, throwing sand and rock into case-mates, and wounding or demoralizing gun crews.

After this bombardment specialized amphibious squads got to work clearing obstructions and at 0630 the first landing craft ran up the beaches. There were five beaches, with General Omar Bradley's US First Army landing at the two most westerly (Omaha

and Utah) and the British, Canadians and Poles, forming the British Second Army, going ashore at three beaches to the east (Gold, Sword and Juno).

Specialized tanks played an important part. The British had devised a flotation system for battle tanks, enabling them to swim ashore. Then there were tanks with flails for detonating landmines, and with large mortars for destroying concrete emplacements. These inventions worked well, except that bad weather on the second-most westerly beach (Omaha) prevented the successful use of the floating tanks. Here the invading infantry of the US V Corps was paralyzed by hostile fire and for a short period was too demoralized to go forward. But by nightfall it, too, was off the beaches and dug in. On the whole, thanks to Allied superiority at sea and in the air, and the thinly held German line, casualties at this stage, the most critical part of the whole oper-

ation, were light. The first waves of troops were able to extend their beachheads inland, making the space so essential for landing the bulk of the forces. Six days after D-Day, over 300,000 men were ashore and the next stage of the plan was put into effect.

Meanwhile things were going badly for the Germans in the rear. At first both Hitler and his generals persuaded themselves that the Normandy landings were only a feint, and held back their reserves to cope with the main Allied landings they imagined would come later. When the truth dawned, moving reinforcements was not easy. As Rommel, and also the navy commander, had pointed out, Rundstedt's concept of a big mobile reserve depended on good communications, and it was good communications that the Allies, and their friends in the French Resistance, had decided to destroy.

The idea of cutting rail links by pinpoint bombing had been adopted by the Allies

Main picture: A week after D-Day, the concrete caissons designed to form a "Mulberry" harbor are taken across the Channel. Although one of the harbors was badly damaged by a storm, this technology maintained Allied supply lines before a usable port could be captured.

Right: A British-manned Sherman tank, spare parts prominently displayed, in Normandy a week after D-Day.

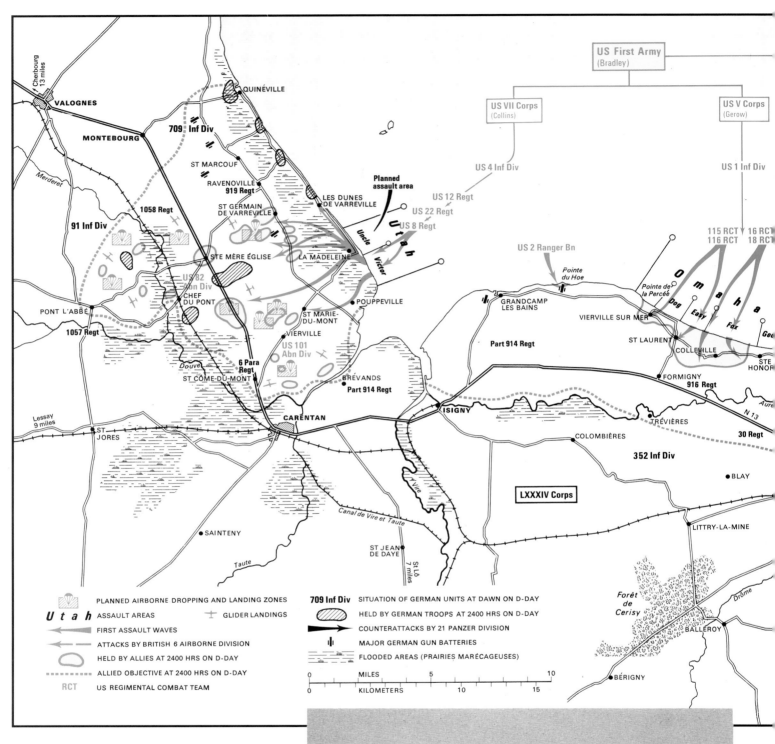

Cherbourg 13 miles
VALOGNES
MONTEBOURG
709 Inf Div
ST MARCOUF
QUINÉVILLE
RAVENOVILLE
919 Regt
LES DUNES DE VARREVILLE
1058 Regt
ST GERMAIN DE VARREVILLE
91 Inf Div
STE MÈRE ÉGLISE
LA MADELEINE
Planned assault area
Merderet
US 82 Abn Div
CHEF DU PONT
PONT L'ABBÉ
1057 Regt
Douve
ST CÔME-DU-MONT
6 Para Regt
Lessay 9 miles
ST JORES
SAINTENY
Taute
Canal de Vire et Taute
VIERVILLE
US 101 Abn Div
ST MARIE-DU-MONT
POUPPEVILLE
BRÉVANDS
Part 914 Regt
CARENTAN
ISIGNY
ST JEAN DE DAYE
St Lô 7 miles
Vire
Uncle
Victor
Utah

US First Army (Bradley)
US VII Corps (Collins)
US V Corps (Gerow)
US 4 Inf Div
US 12 Regt
US 22 Regt
US 8 Regt
US 1 Inf Div
US 2 Ranger Bn
Pointe du Hoe
GRANDCAMP LES BAINS
Pointe de la Percée
VIERVILLE SUR MER
ST LAURENT
COLLEVILLE
Part 914 Regt
FORMIGNY
916 Regt
TRÉVIÈRES
COLOMBIÈRES
30 Regt
N 13
352 Inf Div
LXXXIV Corps
BLAY
LITTRY-LA-MINE
Forêt de Cerisy
Drôme
BALLEROY
BÉRIGNY
STE HONOR
Omaha
Dog
Easy
Fox
Geo
115 RCT 16 RCT
116 RCT 18 RCT

Legend:

PLANNED AIRBORNE DROPPING AND LANDING ZONES
Utah ASSAULT AREAS
FIRST ASSAULT WAVES
ATTACKS BY BRITISH 6 AIRBORNE DIVISION
HELD BY ALLIES AT 2400 HRS ON D-DAY
ALLIED OBJECTIVE AT 2400 HRS ON D-DAY
RCT US REGIMENTAL COMBAT TEAM
GLIDER LANDINGS

709 Inf Div SITUATION OF GERMAN UNITS AT DAWN ON D-DAY
HELD BY GERMAN TROOPS AT 2400 HRS ON D-DAY
COUNTERATTACKS BY 21 PANZER DIVISION
MAJOR GERMAN GUN BATTERIES
FLOODED AREAS (PRAIRIES MARÉCAGEUSES)

MILES 5 10
KILOMETERS 10 15

despite the opposition of Britain's Bomber Command, which believed that precise bombing was impossible. Churchill himself had at one time been persuaded that in order to put French railroad yards out of action tens of thousands of Frenchmen living around those yards would have to die; but he was won over by the Americans and by a few of the more realistic RAF officers. In the event, 10,000 Frenchmen died as a result of these railroad raids, rather than the 40,000 that had been feared.

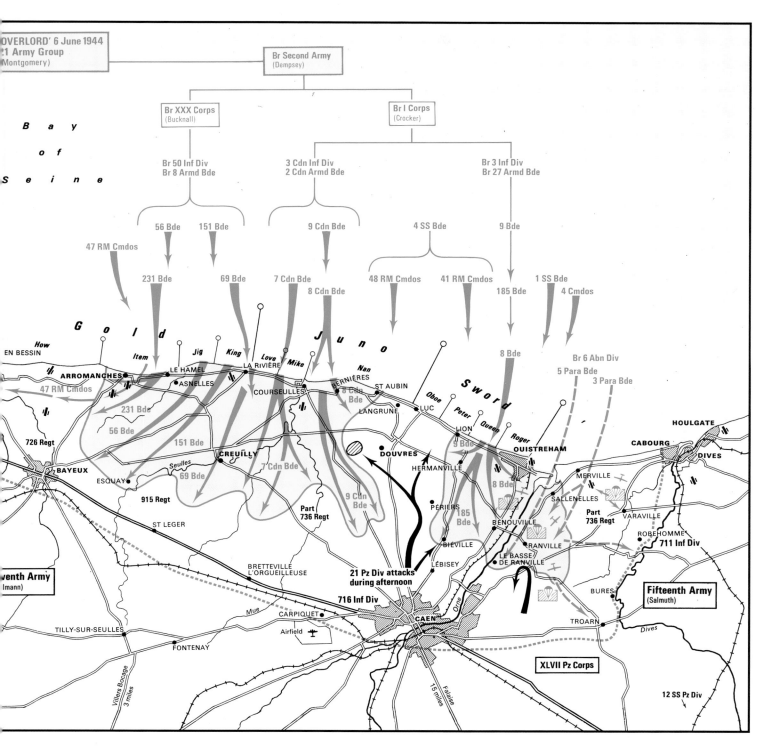

'OVERLORD' 6 June 1944
21 Army Group
(Montgomery)

Br Second Army
(Dempsey)

Br XXX Corps
(Bucknall)

Br I Corps
(Crocker)

Br 50 Inf Div
Br 8 Armd Bde

3 Cdn Inf Div
2 Cdn Armd Bde

Br 3 Inf Div
Br 27 Armd Bde

56 Bde   151 Bde   9 Cdn Bde   4 SS Bde   9 Bde

47 RM Cmdos

231 Bde   69 Bde   7 Cdn Bde   48 RM Cmdos   41 RM Cmdos   1 SS Bde   185 Bde   4 Cmdos

8 Cdn Bde   8 Bde

Bay of Seine

Gold   *Juno*   *Sword*

How
EN BESSIN   Item   Jig   King   Love   Mike   Nan   Oboe   Peter   Queen   Roger

Br 6 Abn Div
5 Para Bde
3 Para Bde

ARROMANCHES   LE HAMEL   LA RIVIÈRE   BERNIÈRES   ST AUBIN   HOULGATE

47 RM Cmdos   ASNELLES   COURSEULLES   8 Cdn Bde   LANGRUNE   LUC   LION   OUISTREHAM   CABOURG

231 Bde   8 Bde   DOUVRES   HERMANVILLE   9 Bde   MERVILLE   DIVES

726 Regt   56 Bde   151 Bde   SALLENELLES

BAYEUX   CREUILLY   8 Bde   VARAVILLE

ESQUAY   Seulles   7 Cdn Bde   PÉRIERS   Part 736 Regt   ROBEHOMME

69 Bde   185 Bde   BENOUVILLE   711 Inf Div

915 Regt   9 Cdn Bde   BIEVILLE   RANVILLE

ST LEGER   LÉBISEY   LE BASSE DE RANVILLE   BURES

Part 736 Regt   Fifteenth Army
(Salmuth)

BRETTEVILLE L'ORGUEILLEUSE   21 Pz Div attacks during afternoon   TROARN

Seventh Army
(Dollmann)   716 Inf Div   Dives

Mue   CARPIQUET   CAEN   Orne

TILLY-SUR-SEULLES   Airfield

FONTENAY   Falaise   XLVII Pz Corps

Villers Bocage
3 miles   15 miles   12 SS Pz Div

Above: The five invasion beaches, with the US landings to the west and the British to the east. Caen's local importance as a road junction is clearly evident.

Left: German coast defense artillery played only a minor role on D-Day.

The raids had lasted for several weeks before D-Day, and by May only a daily average of 32 locomotives had got through to serve the Wehrmacht in France, whereas 100 were needed each day, and many more after the landings. By D-Day, of the 24 rail and road bridges over the Seine north of Paris, only three were still usable, and these three were only passable in the night hours. With freight yards and locomotive depots wrecked and bridges down, the German command was simply unable to move its troops swiftly

to where they were needed. Troop and supply trains, halted by track congestion, were sometimes attacked by French Resistance units.

This paralysis of German communications eased the next phase of the Allied plan. The essence of this was that the British, in the east around Caen, would advance in that area in the expectation of meeting strong German forces which would then be tied down in a hard struggle. Meanwhile Bradley's Americans would concentrate on breaching the line of Germans enveloping their positions, with the aim of creating a gap through which US armored divisions, under Patton, could rush out and threaten the German rear.

The British under Montgomery achieved their aim, although the operation did not start well. Excessive bombing may have driven the remaining Germans out of Caen but also produced acres of rubble that the British forces had difficulty in passing. Further bombing transformed the landscape but failed to find the German tanks. So when the British and Canadian tanks advanced they took heavy losses from concealed enemy armor. Nevertheless, the strength of the British assault persuaded the German command to send four extra armored divisions to the area by the end of June, which meant there were four fewer armored divisions to oppose Bradley when his forces began their sweeping breakout.

Then, in July, Bradley's men were well on the move. With tanks and infantry linked to low-flying fighter-bombers by efficient radio networks, a gap was forced in the German line. On August 1, Patton's Third Army broke out south of Coutances and swung west to Britanny, where it freed the countryside and began to deal with the strong garrisons the Germans had placed in the ports. Soon its main strength was redirected toward Paris.

By this time Rommel had been wounded and Rundstedt dismissed. The new German commander was Kluge, a man not inclined to oppose Hitler's decisions. Already the new command was in trouble. When Patton had broken out, some US tanks had been sent gingerly eastward. Hitler had seen this growing bulge on the map and decided that a German thrust to Avranches would neatly cut it off, after which it could be annihilated by following forces. Kluge obediently scraped together six divisions and sent them west, where they found themselves jammed between Patton's army and the expanding Allied beachheads.

Left: One of the German defenders of Caen, a member of the SS *Hitlerjugend* Division.

Above: Two damaged German tanks, one a Tiger (right) and the other a Mark IV, effectively block the main street of a Normandy town.

Left: Three weeks after D-Day, an antitank section of the Durham Light Infantry takes a look at an immobilized German Panther tank. Another destroyed tank is smoldering in the background.

Top left: The "Watch in the West." German detachments, thinly spread, kept watch along the French coast for months before the Normandy landings.

Top right: The escort carrier USS *Kasaan Bay* is glimpsed through signal flags on the USS *Tulagi* as the Allied invasion of southern France gets under way, August 1944.

Above: Inside a British aircraft as paratroopers await the order to jump at the beginning of the liberation of Europe.

Right: Defenses in depth like these were found on the coast of occupied Europe, but the Allies faced nothing so substantial on D-Day.

Above: German
infantrymen advance
through Caen. The
severity of the British
bombing, which may have
made the Germans
uncomfortable but
certainly made progress
difficult for British
ground troops, is evident.

Left: Under the command
of their sergeant
(extreme right), British
gunners take part in the
preliminary
bombardment designed
to prepare the way for
the assault on Caen. By
this time, enough medium
guns had been landed to
lessen the various armies'
reliance on bombers.

Canadian troops were despatched south from the coast toward Falaise, where they would be met by some of Patton's armored units moving north, and in this way cut off the Germans. This had the effect of pinning the German divisions along a 40-mile stretch of highway, where they were strafed and bombed mercilessly by the USAAF's Thunderbolts, Lightnings, Liberators and Fortresses. A good performance by a German panzer division opened a way of escape from this Falaise Pocket, but losses were enormous. German vehicle losses in this unnecessary disaster were about 2000, and the one-sided battle marked the end of the Normandy campaign. This had gone remarkably well for the Allies. Luck (or rather the absence of bad luck) played a part, but it was a deserved victory nonetheless, for the Allies had deployed intelligent planning, technical ingenuity, and on-the-spot bravery and initiative. Their vic-

tory was not simply a triumph of material superiority.

In one respect the Allies may be said to have had bad luck. This was the weather but, again, the Channel being what it is, the conditions could have been worse. Its high spirits on D-Day had probably advanced the Allied cause, but this could not be said of the storms that raged from 19-22 June. Careful and expensive preparations had been made to keep the invasion force supplied until Cherbourg could be captured; there was PLUTO (Pipe Line Under The Ocean) for supplying motor fuel, and there were the two "Mulberries," sectional concrete jetties that formed temporary harbors at the beaches themselves. The storms wrecked the westernmost Mulberry, badly affecting supplies for the American formations.

Enemy forces had scant chance to attack the Allied supply line. The exception was

Above: One month after D-Day the Allied commanders meet to discuss the next phase of the campaign, and to be photographed. General George Patton, revolver on customary display, is in the foreground as General Omar Bradley looks on, while General Bernard Montgomery, still their commander, manages an affable display for the photographer.

Far left: Going ashore was a tense moment even for those who were not in the first wave. Even so, two of these US infantrymen find the photographer more interesting than the beach.

Left: The Normandy campaign involved much street fighting. For the outnumbered Germans, it was the best way of slowing the Allied advance as a few well-concealed and determined men could create long delays.

Left: American troops, aboard their craft in the tense hours before the invasion is finally launched, do their best to keep smiling.

Above: To accommodate the horde of landing craft, many tiny British harbors were used, but congestion was inevitable. Luckily the German air force was no longer capable of mounting effective raids.

U-boats operating from French ports from June until August. Although equipped with *schnorkels* and therefore immune to radar search, these boats faced overwhelming defensive forces in narrow and shallow waters. Nevertheless they managed to sink 12 freighters and some smaller craft. But the difficulty of their mission was emphasized by the loss of 20 boats out of the original 30.

Despite the crippling of one Mulberry and the delayed capture of Cherbourg, Patton had enough supplies, and in August was rushing onward, toward Paris, while the other Allied armies prepared to cross the Seine and Somme to advance into Belgium.

In the meantime, German problems had been compounded by another assault on occupied France, this time from the south. This, Operation Dragoon, was a relic of the

Left: August 1944, somewhere in France, and a scene repeated daily as isolated German detachments surrendered to the Allies. Here, a German officer surrenders to the Argyll and Sutherland Highlanders, while on the left a local inhabitant, wearing a British army belt and a non-British revolver, offers his help to the major in charge, who is Canadian.

Left: The Germans suffered catastrophically from ground-attack aircraft when they were attempting to struggle through the Falaise gap. The carnage is evident in this picture of the aftermath of an Allied strike taken after the bodies had been removed.

Below left: Another batch of German prisoners is escorted through a French town, Mondeville, in July 1944 by British troops.

inter-Allied wrangling over the time and place of the second front. Churchill had at one time wanted to exploit the Allied successes in Italy and drive into occupied Europe from that direction. When his Allies proved lukewarm, he was persuaded that southern France met his specification for a soft underbelly. The original idea was that the landings (Operation Anvil) should take place simultaneously with the Normandy landings. This would have presented the Germans with enormous logistic problems, but it also presented the Allies with a similar problem; they did not have enough landing craft to stage two landings simultaneously. For this reason the operation did not take place until August.

The advantages of this operation were seen to be the acquisition of two good ports, Marseilles and Toulon, through which could be funneled additional US forces for the fight against Germany, forces that with the existing port shortage in northern France would otherwise have to wait months for deployment. Such troops could move northward, skirting neutral Switzerland, and then turn east into southern Germany.

The German units defending southern France were numerically strong but of low quality. As soon as the Allies had consolidated the landings the German command had the unusual good sense to order a prompt withdrawal, leaving strong garrisons only in Marseilles and Toulon to deny them to the Allies for as long as possible.

Although the US General Alexander Patch was in charge of the Anvil landings, and sea control was exercised from a US command ship, a feature of this operation was the strong French participation. Whereas the French had taken a minor part in the Nor-

Above: US troops on the march close to the shore of southern France. The wall on the right was part of the German defenses, consisting of an eight-foot-high steel and concrete barrier running the full length of the beach.

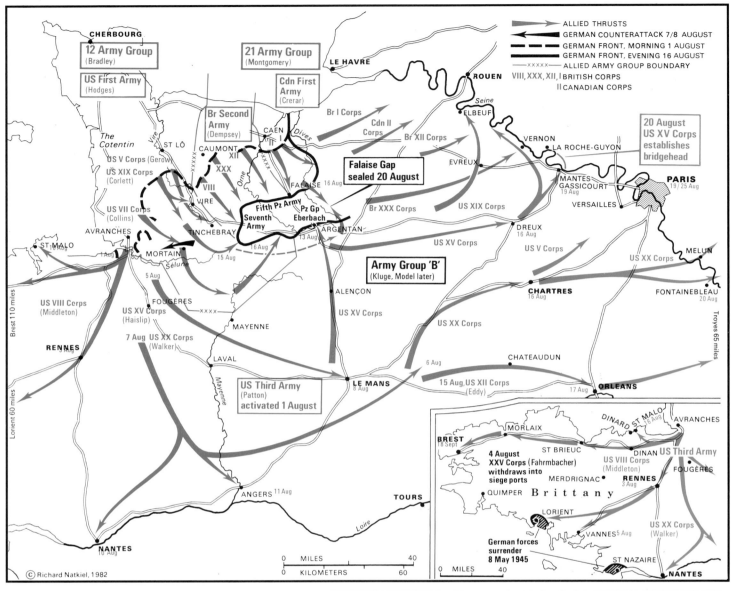

ALLIED THRUSTS
GERMAN COUNTERATTACK 7/8 AUGUST
GERMAN FRONT, MORNING 1 AUGUST
GERMAN FRONT, EVENING 16 AUGUST
xxxxx ALLIED ARMY GROUP BOUNDARY
VIII, XXX, XII, I BRITISH CORPS
II CANADIAN CORPS

12 Army Group (Bradley)
US First Army (Hodges)
21 Army Group (Montgomery)
Cdn First Army (Crerar)
Br Second Army (Dempsey)
Falaise Gap sealed 20 August
20 August US XV Corps establishes bridgehead
Army Group 'B' (Kluge, Model later)
US Third Army (Patton) activated 1 August

© Richard Natkiel, 1982

0 MILES 40
0 KILOMETERS 60

4 August XXV Corps (Fahrmbacher) withdraws into siege ports
German forces surrender 8 May 1945
US Third Army
US VIII Corps (Middleton)
US XX Corps (Walker)
Brittany
0 MILES 40

mandy operations, they were now given a starring part in this, partly because they had impressed the local US commanders. The French troops were less veterans of the old Free French than soldiers of the North African forces who had joined the Allies after the invasion of French North Africa. The military units were largely equipped by the Americans, but the navy had cruisers and destroyers of the prewar French navy.

The operation began on August 14, when 5000 US and British paratroopers were dropped behind the intended beachheads to block all the roads that German reinforcements might take. About the same time, at night, French commandos were landed to capture certain key coastal guns. They were mainly successful, but one group found itself in a lethal minefield, and retreated to the coast where it was strafed by RAF fighters in error, after which capture by the Germans

Left: General Montgomery addresses winners of gallantry medals in Normandy. The censor has blocked out all readable regimental shoulder titles and badges.

was probably a relief. Meanwhile, US Rangers on a similar mission discovered that the guns they had so bloodlessly captured were only wooden dummies. After all this, at dawn, came the bombing and the naval bombardment. Two old US battleships, *Arkansas* and *Texas*, and French cruisers participated in this. The landings went well, except that the German defenses at St. Raphael had withstood the bombardment, so the invasion force simply by-passed this town and took it the next day. By August 17, US troops occupied a broad belt of southern France and were waiting to push north.

The main French forces had not taken part in the first landings, simply because it had been decided that only one language, English, could be used in such a fraught undertaking. But the French First Army under General de Lattre de Tassigny was landed on August 16 and under his gifted leadership and unique zest, born of firing on German strongpoints while simultaneously accepting kisses from the local womenfolk, made rapid progress.

The German garrisons were strongly established in the two ports but, surrounded by a local population that was excited, hostile, and jubilant, could not fight a conventional house-to-house defense. By the end of August Marseilles and Toulon were both in French hands, several days before schedule. US troops had meanwhile been pressing north over two routes, up the Rhône and along the Alps. The latter was entrusted to the US 6th Army Group, made up of the French First Army and the US Seventh. Two weeks later, in September, they would be approaching southern Germany.

Far left: A somewhat reluctant German private, carrying an improvised white flag, is pushed forward as a German detachment surrenders to the Americans in a southern French town east of Toulon.

Above left: The Seventh Army advances north near Montelimar, passing the remnants of an air-stricken German convoy. Some of its horses remain unburied.

Above: A specially-converted Sherman tank designed to explode enemy mines.

TAKE-OFF IN THE PACIFIC

Left: Two Marines make use of a sandy shell hole as they prepare to advance into the interior. This is Saipan in June 1944, but the picture is typical of most of the Pacific island assaults.

As 1944 opened, the best line of approach against Japan had still not been decided. Indeed, at that time there was no need for a decision, because the US had ample resources to continue its two-pronged advance. In the southwest Pacific, General Douglas MacArthur with his Australians and Americans was battling in New Guinea, intending, as soon as he was ready, to advance methodically on the Philippines. In the central Pacific the US Navy preferred its own strategy of moving from island to island until Formosa or China could be reached. Japan's mainland would then be cut off from its main raw materials and be an easier prospect for invasion.

In December 1943 at the Cairo Conference, the US Navy's proposal for continuing the two-pronged approach had been approved. As soon as the navy and Marines had taken the islands of Guam, Tinian and Saipan, Superfortress bombers would be sent to those islands to begin the strategic bombing of Japan itself.

MacArthur would have preferred the allocation of all resources to his own advance, but there were good reasons at that time for rejecting his advice. His line of approach passed through the waters south of the Philippines, commanded by numerous Japanese air bases, and it would have been risky to have used the fast carriers of the fleet in such narrow seas. On the other hand Saipan, as well as providing a good airfield, would make an admirable base for US submarines which, with the benefit of improved torpedoes and painfully acquired experience, were being seen as a very important arm, capable of destroying Japan's vital sea routes and communications.

The Japanese command felt that MacArthur was the greatest threat, and tended to send its best air units to the southwest. The US Navy's operations in the center were greatly aided by this, and in 1944 it repeatedly found itself opposing Japanese pilots who were not fully trained.

In the central Pacific, the Gilbert Islands had already been taken in November 1943, with the amphibious assault on Tarawa having delivered a costly lesson to the Americans. The need for really thorough reconnaissance, and for an assault vehicle that could cope with coral reefs, was now understood. One technical solution was the LVT (Landing Vehicle Tracked), an amphibious personnel carrier whose tracks, armor, and armament gave it some tank-like qualities. Many had been used in the Tarawa operation, and many were lost because the

Japanese had not been quelled by the preliminary bombardment. Despite their heavy losses they had showed how useful they could be and their production rates had been increased.

Benefiting from the experience of the Gilbert Islands, the Americans transferred their attention to the Marshalls, the next step to the northwest and providing jumping-off bases for the ensuing invasion of Saipan and other islands in the Marianas group. These island groups consisted, typically, of one or two major islands and scores of small ones, and the first question addressed by staffs was which islands needed to be assaulted and which could be by-passed. A steady attritional war, taking every island, would take so long that the momentum of the American advance would be lost.

Admiral Chester Nimitz, commanding the US Navy in the Pacific, finally decided that only a handful of the Marshall Islands should be invaded. One was Majuro, undefended by the Japanese but with a good anchorage. Others were Kwajalein and Eniwetok, which were strongly held. These latter two were main bases for the local Japanese air squadrons, but there were other islands with smaller airfields. Boldly, Nimitz decided to

Above: The assault on Roi island in February 1944. The crew of an LST prepare the doors as the craft nears shore.

Above right: Army and navy commanders, and a politician, pictured during the Marshall Islands campaign. The politician (third from left) is Roosevelt's Navy Secretary James Forrestal, and on the extreme left is Admiral Raymond Spruance, overall commander of the Marshall Islands operation.

by-pass these smaller islands. He reckoned their air units could be neutralized by air strikes from his carriers and there was no strategic need to raise the US flag on them; sooner or later, cut off as the American advanced beyond them, they would lose all importance.

Nimitz's Fast Carrier Forces, divided into four task groups, provided most of the action in the first days. Like so many other US fighting formations, this task force had received much new equipment over the preceding months. While still using the big prewar carriers *Enterprise* and *Saratoga*, it had four of the new "Essex" type as well as six light carriers of the "Independence" class. Added to this, in case the Japanese battleships should be encountered at close range, the task force had half a dozen modern battleships in attendance.

In late January these task groups were ranging here and there, raiding numerous atolls in the Marshalls with the aim of destroying, bit by bit, the Japanese aircraft and small naval craft defending the islands. Majuro was duly occupied without trouble, but two small islands, Roi and Namur, proved difficult. Part of the very large Kwajalein atoll, they were surrounded by wide

lagoons across which the assaulting troops had to be carried in boats. Luckily the Japanese had not fortified the landing areas, and casualties were quite light. The three-day bombardment that preceded the landing had not quelled the defenders, and it was a case of dealing with each one, almost man by man. When the islands were finally in US hands they were so devastated that not only were there no surviving buildings, but few surviv-

Above: Pilots of a fighter squadron aboard the aircraft carrier USS *Intrepid* are briefed for the attack on Roi Island.

ing trees either. This was a picture that would become familiar to many troops as the Pacific war progressed.

For invading the much larger Kwajalein Island, the US Navy was determined not to repeat the mistake of Tarawa. No fewer than four battleships were brought up to supplement the bombardment by smaller ships and the aerial attacks. After almost three days of this bombardment, the assault forces went in, in four waves of LVTs. All went according to schedule and was skilfully executed, with the first wave of LVTs unloading and returning through the lines of the advancing second, third and fourth waves. Although landing about 1200 men without a single casualty in the first 10 minutes, the attackers had still not secured dominance. Despite the heavy bombardment, about half the 5000 Japanese defenders, well dug-in, had survived. Using a developed system of trenches, positioned behind antitank obstacles and strengthened by pillboxes and blockhouses, the Japanese put up dogged resistance until they were virtually annihilated.

After a week of fighting for the various islands of Kwajalein atoll the Americans gained control. Casualties were less than had been feared, only 732 Marines and soldiers being killed. Of the nearly 9000 Japanese defenders, about 8000 had been killed.

Eniwetok, the most westerly of the Marshalls, was the next goal. Because Eniwetok was within range of Truk, the Japanese naval and air center, it was decided to raid that island at the same time. So, while the Marines were landing on Eniwetok, the Fast Carrier Force was off Truk. US submarines had been posted outside, to catch Japanese units seeking to escape to sea, but the main naval units had already gone when the US aircraft began their attack. Only a light cruiser was left, and this was sunk by the US submarine *Skate* as it sought the open sea. However, many Japanese transports anchored in the lagoon were sunk. The first target had been the airfields, where almost the entire Japanese aircraft allocation was caught and destroyed on the ground by US fighters and incendiary-dropping Avengers. By the end of the day the Japanese had been able to launch only one, weak, air counterattack, in which the carrier *Intrepid* was damaged by a torpedo.

Then, unusually, the task force indulged in night bombing, with specially fitted Avengers, and the following morning air attacks were renewed with maximum intensity. At the end of this almost continuous bombing, lasting two days, about 200,000 tons of the

dwindling Japanese stock of merchant shipping had been destroyed, as well as over 250 aircraft. For the first time, a major enemy base had been destroyed by carrier aircraft, without the assistance of ground forces or land-based bombers.

Truk would never again be used as the main base of the Japanese fleet; it was too dangerous. This turn of events had taken the imperial command by surprise. Somehow, it had expected that one day Truk would be the Japanese Midway, with the Americans attacking it by sea, meeting the full force of the Japanese fleet, and being defeated. But, as surviving records indicate, wishful thinking played a large role in Japanese planning.

The attack on Truk enabled the US invasion of Eniwetok atoll to proceed without interference from the air. In many ways the landings here presented the same picture as on previous occasions. Going ashore on one of the northern islands of the atoll was relatively easy, the preliminary bombardment having been more successful than usual in devastating the defenders. However, the landings on the two southern islands, Parry and the main island Eniwetok, were less easy than expected. This was because right up to the last minute they were thought to be undefended. Eniwetok proved to be the worst problem, thanks largely to the dense and extensive minefields that the US infantry and Marines had to pass to get at each Japanese strongpoint. In the end the capture of the atoll cost 339 American lives.

This left the Americans in control of all the main atolls of the Marshalls group, although four of those that were by-passed had air-

Above left: A light tank assists US infantrymen as they deal with surviving Japanese on Kwajalein atoll.

Far left: The effect of naval bombardment on Kwajalein atoll.

Left: Another view of the Kwajalein battle. US machine guns cover the advance of infantrymen, who gain further help from the tanks in the background.

Right: Coral and sand in the Marshall Islands. This photograph was taken from a landing craft that had run aground while attempting to land Marines on one of the atolls. The Marines are continuing their voyage on foot, through deep water. This was one of the many atolls that the Japanese chose not to defend.

Below: Daybreak on the beach. A US tank leads a counterattack as one infantryman hurries to find a better position.

fields. It was again calculated that any Japanese aircraft using those fields would be harmless, being more and more isolated from the moving battlefield, and in any case cut off from supplies. Other by-passed atolls had Japanese detachments of only a few men; Bikini, for example, had a Japanese garrison of just five which, in the end, decided to commit suicide.

While island-hopping was getting into full swing in the central Pacific, in the other arm of the American advance, New Guinea, the Japanese were beginning to be thrown off balance by MacArthur's technique of leapfrogging. Essentially this consisted of shore-to-shore landings. Instead of attacking the Japanese defense line MacArthur would embark troops in amphibious craft and land them miles behind the Japanese lines, preferably at a point where they could easily capture a Japanese airfield for their own use. In this way the US and Australian troops avoided big frontal ground assaults, winning considerable terrain with relatively light casualties thanks to their overall command of the air and sea.

Thus in January US troops landed at Saidor, between the Huon Peninsula and Madang. This was at a weakly defended spot midway between the Japanese Eighteenth Army headquarters and the main supply base. This forced the 14,000 Japanese troops to retreat over the mountains where, cut off from supplies, many died from hunger.

Landings had already been made in western New Britain, and in February, simultaneously with the strikes against Truk, a New Zealand division landed on Green Island, about 100 miles east of Rabaul. This latter landing could be regarded as the final operation of the Solomon Islands campaign, that had begun with Guadalcanal in 1942. A little later the Americans captured the Admiralty Islands, providing airfields from which Truk could be bombed if necessary. In New Guinea, the Saidor landings having gained a new foothold, further shore-to-shore operations took the US and Australian forces along the coast in successive landings. These robbed the Japanese of all their airfields and in May the Japanese command ordered the Eighteenth Army to abandon the field and retire to western New Guinea, stipulating that Biak Island, off New Guinea's northern coast, was to be strongly defended.

The importance of Biak was that it offered three airfields and the rare opportunity of operating bombers from them. Biak would bring the US bombers several hundred miles closer to the Japanese. Moreover, should US bombers be able to operate from these fields the big naval battle, which the Japanese command saw as inevitable during 1944, would be weighted in the Americans' favor. For this reason the Japanese navy behaved during these crucial weeks with more than its usual unpredictability.

It had earlier agreed with the army's com-

Right: General MacArthur in Hollandia, New Guinea, surveys the wreckage of Japanese aviation stores caught by a naval bombardment during the Allied advance.

Above: The Saipan operation. Marines under fire crawl up the beach. The central figure is shining wet, because some landing craft failed to quite reach the beach. The distinctive and very useful "Buffalo" armored amphibious vehicles can be seen in the background.

mand that it would concentrate its air power for the defense of the Marianas, where it expected a decisive engagement, and had specifically declared that whatever happened it would not send more aircraft to help at Biak. But that is precisely what it did. As soon as the Americans landed at Biak the navy sent almost 500 planes down from the central Pacific. Symptomatic of the Japanese way of overlooking essentials by this stage, almost all the incoming pilots developed malaria.

Secondly, the navy decided to intervene against the US amphibious landings in Biak, and made three attempts to carry troop reinforcements there under naval cover. The first attempt was cut short because of a false report of US carriers in the vicinity, the second was driven off by the rather weak local squadron of American and Australian cruisers, and the third, in which Japan's two biggest battleships were to deal with the Allied cruisers, was called off because the battleships were needed for the impending naval battle off the Marianas. In the end, it was thanks to the Japanese defending troops that the US forces were denied the use of the Biak airfields for a month.

In the meantime MacArthur was continuing his landing operations and, soon after Biak finally fell on July 2, he was in possession of Sansapor, on the western head of New Guinea; in other words, he now controlled the entire northern coast of the big island.

In the central Pacific, the Marshalls having been taken, US interest was transferred to the Marianas, and in particular to the three main islands of Saipan, Tinian, and Guam. In late February, US carrier aircraft dropped some bombs on these islands and, more important, photographed them; since Guam had fallen to the Japanese in late 1941 photographic reconnaissance had been impossible. Landings on these islands presented great problems, and a final decision, to invade in mid-June, was not taken until mid-March.

Factors leading to this decision were the flow of new ships to the Pacific fleet, and the realization that the capture of those three islands was essential in order to get closer to Japan. Whereas the demands of war in Europe meant that only three Marine and two army divisions were available for the Marianas operation, the European theater,

because of the British navy's strength, had not necessitated the diversion of significant US naval power from the Pacific. On the other hand, the distance of the Marianas from the nearest US advanced base, the recently captured Eniwetok, was about 1000 miles, over which more than 500 ships carrying 125,000 troops and their supplies would have to be carried.

For the Japanese, Saipan was almost part of the homeland, and was a vital piece in their inner defense line. But when, seeing the danger, reinforcements were despatched, it was too late because US submarines were already in place, waiting. After a reinforcing regiment had been wiped out by US submarines, further attempts were abandoned, leaving the Japanese with under 23,000 men on Saipan. By this time they had realized that US amphibious invasions followed a standard pattern, although they had not found a sure way of dealing with them. Essentially, they saw that the Americans relied on an immense material predominance and were able to shell and bombard for as long as the circumstances seemed to demand.

For island defenders, there was a reverse situation, with modest supplies of weapons, and supplies that could not be replenished. This meant that the Japanese had to rely, as previously, on the self-sacrifice of their soldiers, trading lives for material. In Tokyo, the army's fondness for what was slightingly termed "bamboo-spear tactics" was beginning to be criticized, sometimes by some of the more progressive officers. Its manifesta-

tion, as experienced by US Marines battling for beachheads, was the sword brandishing, shouting, and flag-flapping that so often preceded Japanese counterattacks. The latter, though fierce, were never as effective as the accompanying noise and fuss might have suggested.

On the Japanese mainland scientists were enrolled to devise hoped-for "decisive weapons" that could neutralize the US material superiority, but it was already too late, and in place of clever technical innovations came, once more, a human substitute in the form of suicide tactics. The latter, in 1944, would be more correctly termed "suicidal" for it was initially not a case of crashing planes onto targets but of bombing tactics, like skim-bombing, which were accurate but

Top: US flame-throwers were often the only way to overcome Japanese pillboxes, as shown here on Saipan.

Above: A diminutive Japanese mountain gun, captured by the Americans, is tried out against its former owners on Saipan. Such guns were useful not only in mountains, but also in dense jungle.

Above: Marine gunners set themselves up behind an abandoned Japanese truck as they advance into Garapan, the administrative center of Saipan.

could never be strong if only because the Japanese had few light guns for this purpose. But, as the Marines repeatedly found, the Japanese defenses behind the beaches were terrifyingly dense and lethal. The defenders feared naval bombardment above all else – one Japanese account describes officers and men as "living in deadly fear of it." This is hardly surprising, when US ships often came within three-quarters of a mile of the coast. According to Japanese calculations, an elderly US battleship using just half its main batteries had the same effect as 1250 fighter-bombers.

In preparation for the Saipan landings the US Navy's Fast Carrier Forces began to bomb the Marianas airfields on June 11. The seven modern battleships attached to this force were used to bombard Saipan, but got rather poor results, probably because of lack of experience. When the more elderly battleships were brought in they were far more effective, and, while they were firing, frogmen examined the passages into the lagoon that washed the beaches. As elsewhere in this campaign, they did not encounter the kind of small mine and other obstacles that the Germans had used on the Normandy beaches. Once again Japanese military doctrine, reluctant to acknowledge a need for purely defensive weapons, had failed the Japanese army.

gave little chance of pilots surviving. In the same period the Japanese command, like the German, was engaged in a controversy over the relative merits of immediate shoreline defense or weak shore defenses coupled with strong mobile reserves. As with the German command, no clear-cut decision was made, although there was a growing Japanese preference for the construction of defenses in depth.

Shoreline defense was maintained, but it

Two US divisions were landed on eight adjoining landing beaches to the accompani-

ment of light-gun support and rocket attacks by Avengers. The first waves had to face intense fire nevertheless. Hundreds of LVTs hurried back and forth without a collision, to such effect that 8000 Marines were landed in the first 20 minutes. But this success created its own problems. Thanks to the accuracy and intensity of the Japanese guns and mortars, the amphibious vehicles had to drop their troops on the beaches, whereas the intention had been to carry them inland. On the beaches, the Marines had to endure fierce Japanese counterattacks during the night, and it took three days to reach the line that had been planned for the first day.

Meanwhile one of the ubiquitous US submarines had reported that a Japanese carrier force was coming east from the Philippines, and it was clear that this, and another Japanese force reported by another submarine as coming up from the south, were intending to attack the US transports. The local US commander, Admiral Raymond Spruance, decided that the invasion of Guam would have to be postponed and the transports sent east out of the range of enemy carrier aircraft. Accordingly, reserve troops in the transports were landed and the transports, with a small escort, departed while the majority of other naval craft were attached to the Fast Carrier Forces.

While the major units of the US Navy were engaged in the ensuing Battle of the Philippine Sea, the conquest of Saipan continued.

Enough ships had been left to provide an effective naval bombardment without which, the Japanese local commander said, it would have been possible to push back the Americans. Added to the naval guns were continuous air assaults from the escort carriers left behind. In daylight, 36 aircraft were kept in the air over the carriers, ready to move instantly when the soldiers called for a strike. Army P-47s joined in as soon as one of the airfields was secured.

The final annihilation, or self-annihilation, of the Japanese did not occur until July 7. The Japanese land commander as well as the naval commander (Admiral Nagumo, who in better days had commanded carriers at Pearl Harbor and in the Indian Ocean), committed suicide. Hundreds of Japanese civilians, rather than face the disgrace of capture by the Americans, jumped off the nearest convenient cliffs. About 24,000 Japanese soldiers had been killed, but the US Army and Marines had also suffered badly, with over 3400 dead.

Meanwhile the Japanese had fought and lost the naval battle on which they had gambled all. From before the war, a fleet battle that would put an end to the US Pacific Fleet had been an essential part of Japanese military doctrine. Pearl Harbor and Midway had both been born of this anticipation, and neither had ended in quite the way the Japanese command had expected. In 1943 the Japanese navy had not repeated these attempts, not because of lack of will but because of lack of aircraft. In particular, although aircraft production was making up losses, training pilots was not so easy. Even when aircraft became available for training, fuel shortages meant that new aircrew were slow to acquire flying hours.

However, by spring 1944 new air groups were joining the fleet, even though their crews, by US standards, were only half-trained. With striking power restored to its aircraft carriers the Japanese navy command decided to have another go at that decisive naval battle. The objective was to destroy the US Fifth Fleet; that is, the main fleet operating in the central Pacific whose nucleus was the task force known as the Fast Carrier Forces. The first plan was to attract the American fleet into the waters forming a triangle between the Palau, Yap and Woleai islands. These islands would enable Japanese land-based aircraft to supplement the carrier planes. A line of 25 submarines was placed by the Marianas, to report US movements and to make the occasional torpedo attack. Hundreds of naval aircraft were transferred to the

Below left: After an unsuccessful Japanese counterattack to recapture an airfield on Saipan, American soldiers survey the enemy dead.

Below: Near an abandoned dugout, men of the 4th Marine Division engage in close fighting against some entrenched Japanese. The grenade thrown by one Marine is in mid-air, and his companion is about to throw another, already smoking in his hand. Probably grenades will not be enough to solve this problem, and reinforcements will be needed. The picture was taken on Saipan by a Marine photographer.

Marianas and the Carolinas, and their crews were told they were to sink at least one-third of the US carriers.

The Americans perversely failed to be lured where the Japanese wanted them. They were concentrating on their Saipan invasion, and when US submarines reported Japanese fleet movements they did not respond with an immediate lunge into the baited area. They did discover the Japanese line of submarines, and destroyed 17 of them; this was the occasion of the record-breaking exploit of the destroyer escort *England*, which sank six submarines in 12 days.

The Japanese submarines had achieved nothing and by the end of May were in disarray. This, added to the Saipan landings, persuaded the Japanese command to abandon the original plan and to resurrect an existing plan for a conventional naval battle. Except in one category, light cruisers, the Japanese fleet was numerically inferior. In particular, the Americans had seven fleet and eight light carriers, against Japan's five and four, and US air strength, even ignoring aircrew experience, was double that of the Japanese.

Ozawa, the Japanese commander, was a thoughtful admiral and believed that, with luck, he might compensate for his material and human deficiencies. By sacrificing armor and heavy, self-sealing fuel tanks, Japanese aircraft designers had produced machines with a greater range than corresponding US types. In effect, it was risky for US carriers to launch attacks at more than 200-mile range; if they did their crews might not have enough fuel to return safely. For the Japanese, the effective range was close to 300 miles.

With luck and good reconnaissance, therefore, the Japanese carriers could launch their attacks while the US aircraft were outranged. Approaching from the west also gave Ozawa an advantage, for the prevailing wind would enable him to launch and land planes while steaming toward his enemy, whereas the Americans would need to reverse course to launch planes. Another advantage that Ozawa was determined to exploit was the existence of about 100 Japanese land-based aircraft on Guam, Yap and Rota, and he intended to fight his battle within range of them.

US Task Force 58 consisted of four task groups of three or four carriers each, together with a group of seven modern battleships. The latter were intended as an insurance against a surprise visit by Japanese battleships, but in the Philippines Sea battle they remained about 15 miles from the carrier groups, where their heavy anti-aircraft armaments could still make a useful contribution. The Task Force's main role was to protect the Saipan operation, and its movements were restrained by this consideration.

By June 18 both sides knew that a major engagement was impending. Thanks to the longer range of their aircraft, the Japanese reconnaissance reports were fuller than those of the US scouts, but nevertheless Admiral Raymond Spruance had an adequate idea of what Ozawa was doing, although he was not quite sure of where the Japanese were. Ozawa was mainly concerned with keeping his main force of five big carriers at 400 miles from the Americans, so that he could choose when to move in and, still outside American range, launch his aircraft.

On June 19 Spruance was still anxious that Ozawa might evade him and get within range of Saipan but, not knowing the Japanese position and keen to do something useful, he sent off some of his planes to attack Guam. This turned out to be a wise move, for the enemy aircraft there were intended for action against the US fleet. While the US aircraft were engaged in destroying enemy planes here, Ozawa, at last, revealed himself. His carrier aircraft were picked up by radar at about 150 miles and the US carriers immediately began to launch their fighters.

The first wave of 69 Japanese aircraft was reduced to 24 by the end of its attack, and only one bomb hit, fairly harmless, had been scored, on the battleship *South Dakota*. This was followed by a bigger wave of 130 aircraft, of which 98 were shot down, which was equally ineffective. Ozawa's third strike was luckier; most of the 47 planes were unable to locate the Americans and returned unscathed. The fourth wave also failed to locate its target; part found another target and was mainly destroyed, while most of it was destroyed when it attempted to land on Guam.

Meanwhile, although the Americans could not send aircraft to attack the Japanese carriers, submarines were making their own contribution. Just one torpedo from the submarine *Albacore* sank the new carrier *Taiho*, and the older large carrier *Shokaku* was also sent to the bottom by the submarine *Corolla*. At the end of the day the Japanese navy had again lost its air arm, for apart from the two carriers 346 planes had been destroyed against an American loss of 30.

It was not until the next day that the US carriers, proceding cautiously westward, at last located Ozawa's position. He was reported 275 miles away. He was still out of range, but it was already late afternoon so the

decision was made to launch the attack planes and hope for the best on the return leg. Ten carriers launched a total of 216 machines. They caught Ozawa unprepared. Dive-bombers attacked his fleet tankers while torpedoes sank another carrier, *Hiyo*. Ozawa thereby lost another 65 planes.

Only about 20 US planes were lost in the attack, but many more failed to get back to their ships. Even though the Americans took the risk of fully illuminating their vessels, fuel shortage and darkness meant that many pilots landed in the sea unseen. Some were picked up next day, and in the end all but about 50 aircrew were saved.

Intent on covering Saipan, and perhaps too concerned, from the strictly military point of view, with the welfare of his aviators, Spruance did not attempt to pursue Ozawa further. For this he was criticized, but as time passed this criticism seemed to lose its force. Caring for downed aircrew had a military value in itself, being an act benefiting the morale of all. As for Ozawa, he was sufficiently beaten already. Never again would the Japanese navy be able to mount air attacks from its carriers. Not only had it lost three big carriers and almost 500 aircraft, but also about 500 aircrew who, though inexperienced, were the best Japan could muster.

Above left: US fighters, parked vulnerably on a flight deck, survive Japanese bombing off Saipan. By this stage of the war the Japanese aircrew were already far less skilled than their predecessors of 1941, and their attacks on US ships brought them more loss than gain.

Left: A Hellcat takes off in the Marianas operations in June 1944. The light carrier is USS *Monterey*, one of the "Independence" class that were laid down as cruisers but redesigned during construction. She was completed in mid-1943 and, as part of a task group, was engaged in all the subsequent central Pacific operations.

THE SOVIET OFFENSIVE BEGINS

Previous pages: Soviet Voroshilov heavy tanks advance through the steppes. Unlike the medium T-34, the diesel-powered Voroshilov was far from being a shining example of tank design.

Above: The T-34 was probably the world's best medium tank, but only a few were available when Hitler invaded. However, by 1944, when this picture was taken, thousands had been built. These three are moving up to their start line in the Byelorussian campaign.

943 had been a bad year for the German army in Russia. Hitler's earlier insistence on dividing his strength between two main objectives, Stalingrad and the Caucasus, hoping to capture both, simply meant that he captured neither, and at Stalingrad the Germans and their allies suffered perhaps the most crucial defeat of the war. Having lost 200,000 men at Stalingrad the Germans still had two corps at risk in the North Caucasus and much of 1943 had been spent in extricating them with as little loss of ground and men as possible.

Kharkov had been lost in February, although it was recaptured in March. Russian pressure had won enough ground to relieve besieged Leningrad with a singletrack railroad, although a Russian advance to extend this advantage had been held back by Spanish, Dutch, and Belgian contingents of Hitler's army. The German salient at Rzhev had been pushed back, which was really a blessing for it shortened the German line by 200 miles and thereby helped to stabilize the situation, so that by spring 1943 the German retreat seemed to have ended.

However, merely putting an end to the retreat had not been enough. Hitler had decided to reassert his military strength, because after Stalingrad his allies were beginning to lose faith in him. A quiet row had broken out with the Rumanians, because the

Russian breakthrough at Stalingrad had been across a line held by the Rumanian contingent. Rumanians said they had been put in a no-win situation while Germans said the Stalingrad defeat was all the Rumanians' fault; that both were wrong only made the dispute more bitter.

General Franco had requested the return of the Spanish "Blue Division" which had been fighting for the Germans; the Slovakian government decided that the Slovakian Legion should be regarded as ornamental rather than belligerent; and Hungary asked that its three corps on the Eastern Front should be kept away from the fighting areas; in the meantime Hungarian formations ceased to respond to German orders. Even Mussolini was saying that Germany should seek a peace with Russia. In the ostensibly neutral world, Portugal was in the process of declaring against Germany and the Swedish government, hitherto a quiet friend of the Nazis, had begun to hedge its bets.

It was considerations like these that had persuaded Hitler to launch the offensive of summer 1943 that was to be known as the Battle of Kursk. Thanks partly to Russian knowledge of what the Germans were planning, the German attack made little headway before Hitler, in the middle of the battle, withdrew some of his armored divisions to cope with the Allied invasion of Italy. The

Left: Red Army men hurry a heavy mortar into position. These were sometimes used when other armies would have deployed artillery. They were uncomplicated, and had a fast rate of fire.

battle, therefore, far from producing a resounding German victory, was at least technically a Russian victory since it was the Germans who gave up before reaching their objectives. Kursk was also notable in being history's biggest tank battle. After it, German armored strength never completely recovered, a circumstance that was to have a great influence on the events of 1944.

The Germans had always had fewer tanks engaged than the Russians, relying on better quality both of machines and men. But by 1943 this calculation was no longer valid. The disparity of numbers had widened; at the worst point of 1943 the Germans had only been able to muster 500 serviceable tanks on the Eastern Front, for spare parts shortages meant that only a small proportion of the paper strength was active. German tank production was barely sufficient to replace losses, and in some months could not even achieve that. Added to this was the poorer training of the new tank crews. The concept of a replacement army, in which new soldiers could perfect their skills before being directed to a front, had been whittled away by Hitler, who believed that all possible strength should be sent to the front.

There was also a continuing qualitative inferiority. The tanks which had entered Russia in 1941 were technically inferior to the Russian T-34 and KV tanks but those Russian tanks had only just gone into production. But by 1943 almost all Russian tank production consisted of the new types, whereas German industry was still producing slightly improved versions of the old Mark III and Mark IV types. Even with better armor and bigger guns, these were still not a match for the Soviet tanks.

Above: A Soviet light field gun during the Battle of Kursk. Russian artillery had a good reputation, but there was a reluctance to introduce new designs of gun.

In 1943 the Germans therefore changed to two new designs. This change in itself caused a production loss as factories were re-tooled and defects ironed out. However, the new Mark VI Tiger was the most powerful tank in the world until the Russians managed to bring the Iosif Stalin into production in 1944. The Mark V Panther was also a powerful unit, well capable of dealing with the Russian T-34. Both the Panther and Tiger had been used in the Battle of Kursk, but did not do very well, largely because they had not had time for proper assimilation by the armored units. In 1944 they could be expected to outperform the Soviet armor, but they would continue to be scarce and manned by crews whose training and experience were not as good as they could have been.

The situation was worse with motor vehicles. By 1943 some motorized divisions were unmotored. Their officers no longer rode in cars, but on horses, and the men were not in motor trucks, but on foot. Most divisions, motorized or not, were understrength. A division could no longer be counted on to have the fighting capacity of a division. Some divisions remained in being but were at one-third strength or less. This sometimes confused Russian intelligence, which was partly the intention, but it also led Hitler to believe that the Russians were playing the same trick, and that their divisions, too, might often consist of a few surviving companies. This was not so, as the German generals knew quite well, but Hitler nevertheless used this argument when forbidding retreats or urging new counter-offensives.

By the end of 1943 the Red Army was clearly superior in artillery. Indeed, it was probably superior before then; even in tsarist times the Russian gunnery had been very good. It was also distinguished by its use of rocket projectors that fired a pattern of missiles that was far more demoralizing than mortar fire. The Germans had received an improved 75mm antitank gun during the

Russian campaign, and had learned that the 88mm AA gun was also a superb antitank weapon, but they were already beset by shortages. To some extent heavy mortars made up for the gun shortage, but there was also recourse to non-standard artillery previously captured from the French, Czech and Russian forces.

The Battle of Kursk had been followed by a renewed series of Russian offensives. The Germans again lost Kharkov and then the capital of the Ukraine, Kiev. A preliminary Soviet attempt to force the Dnieper with paratroopers failed when they were dropped not only at night but in the middle of a German panzer formation. Paratroopers were not seen again, and Kiev and the Dnieper were tackled by conventional means. Farther south, the Germans remaining in the Crimea were threatened in their rear.

But despite his reverses, Hitler envisaged new offensives in 1944, winning back the ground and prestige he had lost. The Soviet command was also preparing offensives, and had better means of putting its intentions

Below: Russian infantrymen were always noted for their determination and endurance, and this was true in World War II. This is one of a series of pictures distributed in the West and shows Red infantrymen in battle order.

Left: Western munitions shipments to Russia were small in comparison with Soviet production, but included valuable items that were not produced by Soviet industry. This US-built scout car was used as a gun-tractor by the Red Army's artillery service.

into practice. The general Soviet strategy was to make successive offensives on one or another of the fronts that extended from Finland down to the Black Sea, switching the effort from one front to another to keep the enemy continually off-balance. As soon as the Germans were pushed back on one front, adjoining fronts would become vulnerable and were then themselves attacked.

The influx of US trucks, plus increasing Soviet production of vehicles, gave the Red Army a mobility it had not previously possessed. Unlike the Germans in 1941, who used their motorized units to make deep and tactically dangerous penetrations, the Russians command used motorized formations to shift the focus of attacks up and down the front. On the other hand, a few penetrations were made when a railroad could be thereby cut, making even slower the German shift of reinforcements from one threatened front to another.

Frontal attacks using a preponderance of force were still the Soviet tactic. These were

Below: Operating conditions in Russia for the Luftwaffe were difficult, especially in winter. Here, a Heinkel He III, a veteran tactical bomber, is manhandled onto a runway in 1944.

Above: "The retreating Hun" was how this 1944 picture of a German grenadier on the retreat in Russia, standing wearily baggy-eyed amid flames and destruction, was captioned.

general withdrawal, which finally ended the long siege of Leningrad.

To the south, in the center of the line, there was a Russian offensive in February, recapturing Lutsk and threatening the Germans in Galicia. At about the same time the Russians succeeded in encircling eight German divisions south of Kiev, while yet another offensive made advances in the Donets industrial area north of the Black Sea.

March was the beginning of the spring offensive. In the Ukraine the Russian advance was so powerful that the German retreat became disorganized and several supply dumps were abandoned undamaged. By the end of the month the River Prut had been reached and the capture of the railroad junction of Chernovtsy made it virtually impossible for the Germans to shift forces between Poland and the south. The last Black Sea ports were captured, Odessa being abandoned by the Rumanians without a fight.

These advances cut off the Germans in the Crimea. Hitler had insisted that the German Seventeenth Army remain here so as to provide a jumping-off place for a future counteroffensive. Here the Russian plan was to attack over the Perekop isthmus but at the same time send troops over the ice across the lagoons. The latter, it was discovered, had been reluctant to freeze, but the infantry was told to march over them regardless, relying on the shallowness of the water. This worked well, with most men finding a way across just as the Germans defending the isthmus were in difficulties. The landing in their rear convinced the Germans and Rumanians that it was time to retreat into Sevastopol which, however, they managed to hold only until May. This meant that the German Seventeenth Army no longer existed and the Crimea was in Soviet hands, a major victory that fittingly brought the spring offensives to an end.

Although the Russian advances had been substantial, German losses had been smaller than they might have been. This was partly because the Russian command was cautious and did not risk swift changes of plan to take advantages of perceived weaknesses in the German situation. It was also thanks to good German generalship. Von Manstein was only partly successful in relieving two corps cut off in the south, being hampered by blizzards, but in the spring he managed to keep one of his panzer armies, the First, constantly on the move against Russian communications and supply lines, thereby winning time for other formations to retreat. Kleist, the other army group commander, also conducted a very

very costly, but took advantage of the Soviet superiority of manpower while not demanding much skill from local commanders. However, the casualty list was reduced by fairly prompt relaxation of pressure when German resistance stiffened, this being, ideally, the moment when the weight of offensive was shifted from one front to another.

In January 1944, when ice simplified river crossings, there were Soviet offensives in the north around Leningrad, besieged since 1941, and where by that time thousands of civilians were dying daily. Taking advantage of the frozen Gulf of Finland, the Leningrad Army Group crossed over the ice to fall on the left flank of the German Eighteenth Army, while the right flank of the same force was assailed by the Volkhov Army Group which came up from the south across lakes and marshes. After Novgorod and Luga had been recaptured the Germans were forced to make a

fine retreat and, like Manstein, was rewarded by dismissal in April.

In June the Allies landed in Normandy. This meant the transfer of some German strength from the Eastern Front, although not so much as the Russians had hoped. The Normandy front, plus the Italian front, and the need to maintain some strength in all of occupied Europe, meant that less than half the German army was engaged in the fighting on the Eastern Front.

The Russo-German conflict had witnessed less air activity than other German campaigns. Both sides used ground-attack aircraft but, perhaps because the battle line was so long, air attacks were less frequent and less intense and did not decide the issue of land battles.

Although the Luftwaffe had prepared itself for the 1941 campaign against Russia rather better than the army (it had, for example, provided its men with winter clothing in good time) it had not excelled in the technical sense. A service that could draft aircraft from the Mediterranean to the East without winterization deserved to have a low serviceability factor. Even by January 1943 the availability for use of aircraft on the Eastern Front was less than 25 percent, and mechanics still

found themselves frozen to the equipment they were serving because heated repair workshops had not been thought essential.

However, local commanders had made good use of the aircraft that could be put into the air, so that in practice the Russian numerical superiority was not at all as crushing as it appeared. In 1943 the Red Air Force could not be said to dominate the battlefield. Both German and Soviet commanders complained that they received inadequate air support, and both were probably right.

The Red Air Force had been badly handled in the first year of the war. Part of the trouble was that each army had its own air division subordinated to it, and the transfer of air strength to where it was needed was difficult, with two many levels of command needing to be consulted. A new system had eventually been introduced, based on the air army, whose commander was directly subordinate to the army group commander, who could order redeployment of aircraft within the area of his own front. Redeployment between fronts (army groups) could be ordered by the *Stavka* (the supreme headquarters, chaired by Stalin). The system was perfected when each air army commander sent a deputy with staff officers to work directly

Above: The standard Soviet light machine gun, like the rifle, was well-designed and no more liable to breakdown than similar weapons of other armies.

Above: Red Army snipers in an unlikely situation. Except on the steppes, Russian terrain provided a wide choice of cover and so did war-shattered urban areas. Like so many other pictures of the time, this is plainly a posed photograph.

with the army HQ near the front line. Better response to requests for air support was thereby achieved.

The Red Air Force, like the German, was primarily regarded as an adjunct of the army. Stalin, not without bloodshed, had put an end to ambitions for a strategic bomber force during the 1930s. However, a few months after the war started the Russians had set up an organization far superior to that of the Luftwaffe, in that it preserved the primacy of ground support yet at the same time did not allow the demands for ground support to strangle other roles. They did this by placing directly under the *Stavka* four specialized forces: aircraft maintenance was one, but equally important was the strategic reserve which was intended as a pool from which aircraft could be sent to crucial fronts.

There was also a fighter force modeled on Britain's Fighter Command, which had so impressed the Russians in 1940. Finally, *Stavka* had a relatively small strategic bomber force intended for special missions at the front; this force had no really effective strategic bombers and made-do with smaller aircraft until US bombers were acquired. To ensure that aircraft serviceability remained high, maintenance and supply specialists were given high ranking at each level of air force administration, thereby ensuring that their views would be given due weight.

The strategic reserve had great significance, and at times held two-fifths of the available aircraft. Stalin had a much better appreciation than Hitler of the importance of air reserves. By 1944 the staff had gained experience and confidence in the use of this reserve, which enabled superior force to be concentrated at points where it was important. This had a great benefit in the several offensives of 1944, where the Red Army advanced under conditions of Russian local air superiority. The Luftwaffe had used a similar technique in the Blitzkriegs of 1940, but had been forced to abandon it when aircraft shortage led Hitler and Goering to virtually dispense with a reserve.

The Soviet method had been assimilated quite painfully. In 1942, because Stalin had considered the German advance toward the Caucasus as only a feint, he had not sent aircraft reserves there, which enabled the Luftwaffe to cause serious damage to the Red Army. But in the 1943 fighting in the Kursk salient, *Stavka* was able to allocate 2000 of its aircraft, whereas the Luftwaffe could only put 400 in the air. There were times when Soviet fighters outnumbered German by 10 to one.

The role of the air force in the Soviet ground offensives was expressed in big initial attacks on enemy airfields and supply dumps. Soviet fighters had a certain freedom in choosing targets on the occasions when they were not ordered to cope with enemy aircraft. On average, they spent about a third of their air-time dealing with enemy aircraft, either on the ground or in the air. The bombers were largely directed against German troop formations near the front; attacks behind the immediate front area were rare, partly because the front was quite shallow, with German strength and supplies not dispersed very far in the rear, and partly no doubt because deeper inroads would have resulted in heavy aircraft loss.

However, the Luftwaffe itself soon learned the advantage of deploying in depth and, like the Russians, built secondary or reserve airfields well behind the front. In its turn, the Red Air Force copied German tactics, and the new Soviet manuals for fighter interception and for ground support to a large extent followed what had been discovered about German practices.

By 1944, Soviet aircraft were not only being produced in greater number than German but were also qualitatively superior. Whereas the Luftwaffe had only managed to introduce the FW 190 and improved versions of the Me 109, the Russians had more or less ceased production of older types and were building the celebrated Ilyushin Il-2 "Stormovik" ground-support aircraft and a vastly improved Yak fighter. The German HS 129 aircraft, whose tank-destroying virtues had been demonstrated in the Kursk battle, was produced in only small numbers because of the priority that had to be given to fighters. The "Stuka" dive-bomber, that had been so devastating in 1940 and 1941, was kept in production even though it had become outclassed. In 1944, the Luftwaffe scraped the barrel and even sent biplanes to the front.

The Luftwaffe was hampered by its commitments elsewhere. One of the more solid justifications for British and US strategic bombing of targets in Germany was that this not only slowed down German production but also compelled the Germans to devote a large part of their fighter strength to home defense. In addition, the West was sending new aircraft to Russia. This had started with British Hurricane fighters despatched early in the war which the Soviet regime, predictably enough, regarded as inferior aircraft. But by the end of the war about 14,000 US-built aircraft had been sent to Russia.

By the end of 1943 it was clear that the Luftwaffe was fighting a losing battle on the Eastern Front. Because it was short of aircraft, it had to gradually implement a policy of reserve manipulation, concentrating all available aircraft at certain crucial places, which meant that large lengths of the front were uncovered. And even in the areas where it did concentrate, it was vastly outnumbered by the Russians. In January 1944 the Russians had about 13,000 aircraft available for front-line use, which was three or four times more than the Germans had.

Russia had a few obsolescent four-engine bombers (Pe-8) and these were used mainly against troop concentrations. A Russian bombing attack on Berlin and a few other such sorties were done for publicity purposes and had negligible effect. Later, the Il-1 bomber had been put into production to replace the Pe-8, but it too was used mainly for army support. Hitler, meanwhile, having discovered that Russia was not going to be an easy victory, had spoken of bombing the Urals but had no suitable aircraft, and despite great, if ill-organized, efforts, this deficiency was never remedied.

Right: German troops on the retreat in the Crimea. Hitler was very reluctant to abandon this peninsula, partly because it provided a short-cut to the coveted Caucasus.

BURMA AND CHINA

Previous pages: "Merrill's Marauders," US jungle warfare specialists, photographed in northern Burma during 1944.

Above: British General Orde Wingate of the "Chindits" briefs US aircrews. Flying Dakotas, the Americans were helping to supply remote detachments in the Burmese jungle.

The campaign in Burma, fought mainly by British and Indian troops, was almost the forgotten front of the war against Japan, but it would witness in 1944 the biggest defeat suffered by the Japanese army. Farther north, in China, there was a confused war in progress as two Chinese commands, the nationalist and the communist, maneuvered against each other as they both fought the Japanese. The nationalists, who could claim to be the legitimate rulers of China and who had been fighting ever since the Japanese invaded in 1937, received support from the US.

This support included valuable supplies sent originally over the Burma Road and, after the route had been cut by the Japanese, by air from northeast India. The air lift had at first been part of the role of a very irregular air force, the Flying Tigers, consisting mainly of American volunteers, but by 1944 this had been formalized as the US 14th Air Force and was also carrying out bombing missions, although it was for long held back by shortages of aircraft and spares. American army personnel were present in China as instructors, and US General Joseph Stilwell had virtually created the US-pattern Chinese Army in India, which operated in northern Burma. In China proper US airfields were built, from which not only the Japanese army in China, but also targets sa and Japan itself, could be bombed.

In 1942 the British Commonwealth troops had withdrawn painfully from Burma, being no match for the Japanese in jungle fighting. Their morale was low, they were poorly supplied, and in 1943 had to turn their attention to maintaining order in India proper, where the nationalists were agitating against British rule with various forms of civil disorder. Some of the more militant nationalists even enrolled in an anti-British Indian national army fighting alongside the Japanese.

Nevertheless, having built a defensive line on the India-Burma border and supposing that the Japanese would advance no farther, the British were slowly able to reorganize themselves. The general who had directed the evacuation from Burma, William Slim, and who at the time received no thanks from his superiors, was slowly recognized as a vary capable, if unassuming, leader and in due course became commander of the British Fourteenth Army on the border.

Slim's obvious care for his men made him a popular leader. He had not risen to the top by going to the prestigious Sandhurst Academy but had reached the top by merit in the interwar Indian army. He was a Birmingham man and had a Birmingham matter-of-factness which saw things as they were, and one of the things he had seen was that the Japanese had seemed so superior in Burma because the British had been so unnecessarily bad.

This was something that Slim could change. For example, he trained his men to make oblique advances, so necessary in the mountainous jungle. The Japanese tactic, repeated over and over again, of demoralizing an enemy strongpoint by infiltrating into its rear and then building bunkers that suggested that the defenders were cut off, was soon mastered by Slim. The defenders, he instructed, should not assume all was lost and abandon the position, as they had in the past. They should realize that it was the Japanese behind them who were cut off, so long as the strongpoint was held. Taking a leaf from the Japanese book, Slim insisted that in jungle warfare the specialist technical troops, usually regarded as non-combatant, would have to do their share of the fighting.

Meanwhile, other evidence that the Japanese could be defeated in the jungle came from the exploits of the "Chindits." These were regular soldiers operating in guerrilla style behind Japanese lines in Burma. Under the command of the unorthodox General Orde Wingate, they had quite heavy losses, did not do great damage, but they did from time to time defeat the Japanese. As there was a tendency to regard the Japanese solider as a superman, this demonstration that he certainly was not came as a useful boost to morale. In northern Burma, close to China, "Merrill's Marauders" were the US equivalent of the "Chindits," and would play a great role in the Myitkyina operations in May 1944.

At the start of the war the Japanese high command had realized the importance of Burma, but was surprised that it was overrun so easily. It had given no thought as to what should come next, or how far it should go, which is why it settled for the Indo-Burmese frontier as a finishing line at least until it had made its mind up. For a time there was ambitious talk of pushing on and joining up with the Germans, who both in Egypt and the Caucasus seemed likely to defeat their enemies and have a clear road into Asia.

In March 1943 the appointment of a new commander of the Japanese Fifteenth Army in Burma coincided with incursions by Wingate's "Chindits" that seemed at one time very dangerous to the Japanese position, and which were blocked only with difficulty. Seeing this, the new commander, General Renya Mutaguchi, came to believe that the only way to prevent a repetition would be to advance into India and occupy the bases from which the British operated. Mutaguchi was a self-confident, aggressive man and he managed to persuade his command that the shorter defensive lines that the command had ordered for all fronts would not be suitable for the Burma front. An advance would be the safest form of defense, he said.

The Japanese high command was swayed by another argument. A provisional Indian government was waiting under Japanese protection, composed of anti-British Indian nationalists, and invasion across the border would gain a patch of Indian territory in which this new government could proclaim itself the real government of India. The Southern Army, of which Mutaguchi's Fifteenth Army was a part, did not at first really approve but, pressed between his confident plans and the optimism of the high command, its commander kept his thoughts mainly to himself. In the Fifteenth Army's staff there was an unspoken assumption that the chances of success would not be talked about and that the operation would certainly take place.

Southern Army, finally convinced by Mutaguchi's optimism, then found itself pressing the virtues of the plan on the high

command, which had grown doubtful. Tokyo put some pointed questions about whether the conquered territory would mean more forces would be needed for defense, whether the planned ground operations could be carried out in the absence of command of the air, and whether the rear could ensure the required flow of supplies. The proposed operation, Southern Army now claimed, would actually reduce the number of men required to defend Burma. Convinced, the high command issued final instructions for this "U-go" offensive in January 1944.

In late 1943, when Slim was merely the commander of a corps, the British had launched an attack on the Japanese in the

Above: "Chindits" on the move in Burma, 1944, with the luxury of a pack-mule to carry their equipment.

Below: A view of the terrain near Kohima, which shows why the battle consisted of small engagements between company-sized units.

Arakan hills, hoping to re-take Akyab with its port and airfield. The British corps involved was not Slim's, and had not benefited from the type of re-think that Slim had imposed. It was soon stopped in its tracks. Slim had been sent to take a look at the situation, but his recommendations appear to have been more resented than noted.

However, when things got worse he was given control of the Arakan troops and was able to withdraw them before they were completely demoralized, a feat for which he was strongly criticized by his immediate superior who, however, was soon dismissed. In the promotions that followed Slim became commander of the whole British Fourteenth Army.

At the beginning of 1944, Slim was simultaneously reorganizing the Arakan operation and preparing an offensive of his own style. The latter was to be launched from the forward British supply base of Imphal, just inside India. Slim was soon aware of the impending Japanese offensive, but argued that it would nevertheless be best to continue preparing for his own. Meanwhile, he was on the point of winning in the Arakan where the Japanese, infiltrating behind two Anglo-

Indian divisions, discovered that the British no longer panicked at this maneuver. The Anglo-Indians held on to their positions, Slim airlifted reinforcements and, as he had predicted, it was the Japanese who faced cut-off and had to retreat. In March the British XV Corps was ready to march on Akyab, but had to give up this goal when it was needed by

Above: A key event in the Kohima operations – the Durham Light Infantry link up with an Indian division on the Imphal-Kohima road.

Above: The remains of a village that was fought over in the Kohima battle. Despite the ferocity of the fighting, several huts survive, largely because small arms and grenades were the main weapons.

from the purely strategic and tactical points of view. He took guns no larger than 75mm, probably because that was the biggest gun suitable for elephant transportation, even though the Anglo-Indian forces had quite heavy artillery and some tanks. He made no plans to assemble vastly superior strength at the strategic strongpoints but relied on the old tactic of encirclements by infiltration and temporary strength at crucial local points. Moreover, the plan was rigid, with no provision for alterations in the light of events.

The Allied defense system was based on what the Japanese called "beehives." These were circles of strength, scattered close enough for mutual fire support. At the center of each circle, or beehive, were guns in protective emplacements, and tanks were placed around the guns to act as pillboxes. This defensive system, plus the support of aircraft which both dropped supplies and attacked the Japanese guns endeavoring to knock out the beehives, was extremely hard to break.

The Japanese troops, complete with elephants and oxen, crossed the Chindwin in March. This was somewhat earlier than Slim had expected, and he had difficulty in withdrawing some advanced units to the main positions. The immediate Japanese objective was Kohima, a town on the main road that connected Imphal with Dimapur.

Using their old tactics, the Japanese infiltrated to the rear of the British and in April built fortified roadblocks behind both Imphal and Kohima. They had learned nothing from their recent discomfiture in Arakan, and were surprised when the British did not withdraw after the roadblocks were built.

Admiral Louis Mountbatten, supreme commander in the theater, allocated all available transport aircraft to Slim, and a fleet of Dakotas succeeded in airlifting the division in Arakan back to Imphal in mid-March. The Japanese command had counted on this division being too far away to participate in the battle. On the other hand, partly because he was poorly provided with intelligence, Slim also made miscalculations. One was of a kind frequently made by the British, assuming that the enemy would behave rationally. In this case Slim assumed that the Japanese would send no more than a regiment to attack Kohima, on the grounds that the roads were so bad that supplies could be maintained only for a regiment. In reality, Mutaguchi sent not a regiment but a division to Kohima, and the gap between the requirements and the supplies that could actually be sent was filled by wishful thinking.

Slim's second miscalculation was that the

Slim to help in the defense against the Japanese onslaught on Imphal.

The Japanese began their Imphal operation in mid-March. The characteristic of this long drawn-out battle was that it was fought over a very large area, about 100 miles north to south, yet consisted mainly of a succession of small-scale close-quarter combats. Although on paper it was three Japanese divisions attacking three British divisions, in the battles the basic infantry unit, it turned out, was the company.

Mutaguchi had solved the supply problems to his own and his staff's satisfaction. Three weeks' rations was declared sufficient on the grounds that the operation would last only three weeks. All officers and men were to set off loaded down with the maximum possible weight of supplies. Elephants and oxen were to be recruited and the oxen, on delivering their supplies, would then be eaten. In case all this was not enough, the soldiers had been shown the best ways of eating grass.

Apart from the absurd optimism of his supply arrangements, and his decision to ask for air force support only for the crossing of the Chindwin, Mutaguchi's plan was defective

Japanese were aiming at Kohima in order to push on to the vital railroad at Dimapur, along which passed the supplies that were destined for the US airlift into China. However, the Japanese objective was limited to Imphal. After sending reinforcements to Dimapur, Slim realized his mistake and at the last minute managed to send an extra infantry battalion to Kohima.

Slim, after all, had been presented with the situation he wanted. The Japanese had entered a battle on his own, well-prepared territory and whereas he had air and land links to the rear the Japanese had shaky supply lines that would be unable to transmit all that they needed.

The 11-day climax at Kohima began as a siege but ended in a series of actions fought for a high ridge and a tennis court. Fierce small-scale attacks and counterattacks followed each other, or were sometimes simultaneous. In the struggle for the tennis court, and elsewhere, the British, Gurkha, and Indian companies relied heavily on hand grenades, so close was the fighting. Meanwhile Slim was accumulating about 100,000 men in the Imphal area.

Unwilling, as usual, to give up, the Japanese continued their siege of Kohima far longer than was wise. They had an excuse though. In all appearance they had captured Kohima already, and the fighting that continued was mistaken for mopping-up operations. On about April 6 the Japanese considered that they had captured Kohima, and some of their troops pushed ahead toward Imphal. But in mid-April a brigade of British infantry marching from Dimapur relieved the supposedly captured Kohima. The truth of the matter, as neither side could quite see at the time, was that most of Kohima had been occupied by the Japanese, but there were enough strongpoints still heroically holding out to prevent the whole town falling into the hands of the attackers.

On the plains of Imphal the Japanese, with their standard siege operations, had little success against the beehive defense. And while the attackers were desperately short of supplies the defenders were resupplied daily by air. The rain began in May, so the Japanese operation became both literally and metaphorically bogged down. Mutaguchi responded to this by dismissing the commanders of two of his divisions, claiming that they lacked fighting spirit. These dismissals did nothing to reduce hunger and sickness, nothing to provide needed ammunition, and nothing to deal with British tanks.

Mutaguchi then summoned his 31st Divi-

sion, which "evacuated" Kohima and was instructed to cooperate with the remnants of another division for a final desperate assault on Imphal. Sato, the commander of that 31st Division, was the only divisional commander to have escaped dismissal, which perhaps represents yet one more error of judgment on Mutaguchi's part. For Sato was now fed up, and believed that if he accepted any more orders from Mutaguchi his division would be destroyed. So, a simple man, he did a simple thing – he cut off all radio links with Mutaguchi's HQ. Then, as he had no orders from above, he used his own initiative and took his men back across the Chindwin to the supply dumps just inside Burma. He then sent a message to the area headquarters which said, among other things, that the tactical ability of Mutaguchi's staff lay somewhere below that of raw cadets.

Top: Gurkhas near Imphal. With the Japanese only half a mile away, they are busily cutting and aligning bamboo stakes for use as defense obstacles.

Above: A British Bren-gun carrier with improvised floats negotiates a Burmese river during the drive toward Mandalay that brought the Burmese campaign virtually to an end.

Above: A British tank near Imphal. With tracks like this the Japanese tactic of building fortified roadblocks in the rear of their enemy is understandable.

about 30,000 Japanese dead, and by the time the remnants of his army were back behind the Chindwin, total casualties were about 65,000. This was an enormous shock for the Japanese army, for although in the Pacific it had been ousted from a succession of islands its casualties in any single battle had not been on this scale. Mutaguchi was soon dismissed, but the new commander, like the old, did not introduce new tactics even though it was plain that the old ones no longer worked.

Meanwhile the British and Indians of the Fourteenth Army were reorganizing and re-supplying, and in December 1944 Slim advanced across the Chindwin in an offensive coordinated with Stilwell's Chinese army in the north. After more than two years' experience of fighting the Japanese, Slim correctly divined that they would try to rout his army at the Irrawaddy crossing at Mandalay, and forestalled this by moving unexpectedly against Meiktilla, which commanded the road and railroad to the city and port of Rangoon. The Japanese, alarmed by this move, sent reinforcements to Meiktilla from Mandalay, thereby enabling Slim to capture both these centers. Just before the monsoon broke, Slim's army was in Rangoon and the Japanese were on the run.

While the Imphal battle was still raging the Japanese had been in trouble elsewhere in Burma. In the north, Stilwell's Chinese army was active, and in May, beginning with glider landings, the Japanese found themselves attacked in Myitkyina. They held out until August, but a division sent north to help them was slowly ground down to almost nothing as it advanced. With defeat both in the north and in the west the Japanese forces in Burma were instructed to limit their objective to preserving southern Burma and interfering with the flow of Allied supplies from India into southern China, but they failed in both these missions and would be pushed out of Burma in 1945, taking with them the sorry remnants of the Indian National Army.

On the other side of the Burma-China frontier there was the American 14th Air Force, which had added strategic bombing to its responsibilities for the air link with India. But in early 1944 its bomber operations were hindered because the Japanese, aware of their potential, launched a ground offensive toward the airfields and captured many of them. But later in 1944 the 14th Air Force was organizing heavy bombing raids of Japanese targets in China and also on Formosa. In due course, when more big bombers became available, it would also attack the Japanese mainland.

By this time Slim had decided that his priority was no longer the defense of the Imphal area, but the destruction of the Japanese forces. Mutaguchi and the area headquarters both realized that U-go had failed, and there could be no further progress in the rainy season. But neither wanted to drop their offensive stance and it was only in early July that the high command had the moral fortitude to impose a withdrawal. So, harried from time to time from the air, and occasionally by tanks and paratroopers, the Japanese conducted a retreat, an operation for which they were neither properly trained nor psychologically prepared. As the soldiers trudged back, hungry and sick, they dropped their weapons by the wayside, but held grimly on to their mess kits. They were no longer fighting men.

In total, Mutaguchi's bright idea had cost

ITALY

Previous pages: A US tank pushes inland, but not very far, from the beachhead at Anzio, where the Allies had skilfully put themselves in an unpromising situation.

Left: Allied landing craft under air attack at Anzio. Naval losses were quite high here, with the Luftwaffe taking advantage of a situation in which its enemy kept ships well within reach of its airfields and its observers.

Below: US troops advance slowly through newly gained ground. The dry heat and dust, plus the constant vigilance demanded against snipers and booby-traps, made this advance arduous.

The peculiarity of the Italian campaign was that while it involved huge armies, tough fighting, and territory that was close to Hitler's heartland, it was destined to remain a sideshow. For most of 1944 the size of the German and Allied forces engaged made it second only to the Eastern Front, yet it never really seemed to be a crucial battlefield, except to the Italians themselves.

The British would have preferred to devote more resources to this campaign, on the grounds that this would divert German strength from France. Undoubtedly Hitler saw the dangers of an Allied advance which, having won Italy, might then continue into Austria and southern Germany. In this respect Hitler's and Churchill's strategic views coincided. But the Americans, who would have to supply most of the extra troops if the Italian campaign was given priority, thought differently. Rightly or wrongly, they saw in Churchill's advocacy of the Italian campaign just one more of his ploys to delay the Normandy landings, and they were firmly convinced that the key to victory in Europe was to be found in France, and not in any of the backwaters and underbellies that so fascinated Churchill.

In retrospect, it is clear that the concept of drawing German reserves by a vigorous

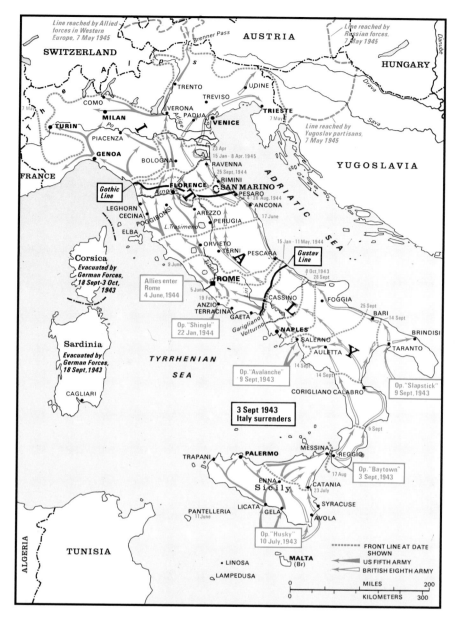

Italian campaign was flawed from the start, for some very basic reasons. The long leg of Italy, mountainous except for coastal strips, was ideal country for defenders. The Allies would have to fight for every yard, and the terrain provided the defenders with some protection against Allied air power. Added to this was that invariable factor of military calculation: attackers need more men that defenders. This being so, it should have been as clear then as it is now that the number of German divisions drawn into the Italian campaign would never be many more than the Allied divisions sent to that front.

These strategic-geographical imperatives could only have been by-passed if German generalship had been abysmal, or if some unexpected stroke, or piece of luck, changed the picture. As for generalship, Kesselring was a highly competent officer who may even

have approached greatness in his steady rearguard action in Italy. He knew where to make a stand, and he knew precisely when to withdraw and, more important, where he should withdraw to. The Allied generals were good, but good generalship could only produce a slow advance, which for the most part devoured more men and materials for each yard of territory than the Germans themselves expended.

In late 1943 the Allies had at last captured Naples and restored its port, but it would take them eight months to push from Naples to Rome, a distance of only about 100 miles. They had control of the adjoining seas and dominance in the air, yet they averaged only a quarter-mile per day.

As for unexpected strokes, Churchill was all too anxious to repeat his 1915 Gallipoli drama, if only to show that the 1915 concept

Top: US troops on the march in Italy survey the remains of a Tiger tank.

Above: "Berlin or bust," painted on the side of this light reconnaissance vehicle, was one of the most common slogans adopted by US troops.

Above left: The Italian campaign.

had been right after all. A powerful landing behind the enemy's main defenses was Churchill's prescription. The Allied advance at the end of 1943 was held up by a strong defensive position that the Germans had built across Italy, the Gustav Line, which made skilful use of two rivers and the virtually roadless central mountains. This line was especially strong in the western sector, where Monte Cassino and two other mountains dominated the area. The US Fifth Army of General Mark Clark had been moving toward this western sector of the line since October, but after costly fighting only reached it in time to come to a halt as the bitter, high-altitude, winter closed in. The Line itself, evidently, was not going to be an easy problem for the Americans. At the eastern end the British Eighth Army, facing fewer mountain obstacles, had broken the Line at the coast. Or rather, so skilful was Kesselring, had not broken it but pushed it back a dozen miles.

Churchill persuaded the Combined Chiefs of Staff (the highest Anglo-American planning group) to make an amphibious landing behind Kesselring's Gustav Line. Anzio was the beach chosen, just 37 miles south of Rome and about 50 miles northwest of the Gustav Line. Operation Shingle, as it was called, would aim at initially landing one or more divisions that would seize the high ground beyond the beaches. In the meantime Clark's Fifth Army would advance past Monte

Above: US infantry rest in the shelter of a drainage ditch near Anzio. This picture has a certain symbolism, given the unaggressive Allied stance at this time and place.

Left: Eisenhower and General Mark Clark leave a frontline conference in Italy.

Cassino to link up with the Anzio forces at a road junction in the hills.

The Fifth Army began its advance in early December, but it soon became clear that the town of Monte Cassino would take longer to subdue than anticipated. The Germans had wasted none of the weeks they had waited there, and the town, monastery, and surrounding terrain were honeycombed with tunnels and other earthworks that defied the efforts of Allied gunners and pilots to dislodge the defenders.

This hold-up made the Anzio landings a doubtful proposition, because the relatively few Allied units at the beachhead would no longer be able to rely on Clark's Fifth Army fighting its way to link up with them before the Germans could deploy massive strength against them. Wisely, the Allied command canceled the Anzio operation but then, at the instigation of Churchill, it was restored. It thereby became yet another of those Allied initiatives, adopted for a set of circumstances, which was carried out even though those circumstances never developed.

Having strong naval gunfire support, and achieving tactical surprise, the Anzio landings of January 22 were successful, the troops merely being ferried from Naples in landing craft. Once ashore, however, the question arose of what to do next. At first there was one US and one British division ashore, but the balance altered when reinforcements, almost entirely American, landed. In the end the Anzio affair became an operation whose concept was British but whose execution was largely American, and this was fertile soil for controversy later, when it was realized that the landings had been a sheer waste of resources.

The US general on shore, John P. Lucas, was blamed for concentrating on defending his beachhead, rather than pushing into the hinterland to broaden his front and envelop the Germans on the nearby hills. But Lucas was too weak to do this without inviting disaster. The Allies, moreover, had underestimated Kesselring's ability to shift his troops at short notice, a mistake that was compounded by the British and US air forces'

Above: A US tank, safely out of range, overlooks the town of Cassino. The picture shows how the way north was dominated by the high ground, and why the Germans and Allies fought so long and destructively for it.

Above: Another view of the Cassino battle, with Monastery Hill in the background.

Right: A British soldier in action amid the rubble of Cassino. He is using a Bren-gun, the Czech-designed light machine gun that served the British infantry throughout the war.

Above: German paratroops, no longer used as such, defending the line in Italy.

Above right: General Sir Harold Alexander, the ever-patient commander-in-chief of the Allied forces in Italy, photographed at his HQ in 1944.

claims to have destroyed key bridges that, in fact, remained in place for Kesselring to use.

Kesselring was able to hold the US Fifth Army and the British Eighth at his Gustav Line, while sending some of his reserves against Anzio. So what had started as a surprise Allied thrust soon developed into a desperate Allied effort to save the beachhead. Saving the beachhead had little strategic benefit but had become important simply for morale.

Thanks largely to gunfire support from British, US and French cruisers and destroyers, the defenders of the beachhead did hold out. But it was at a high price. The Luftwaffe, though weak, did have a few of its glider bombs available, and German observers in the hills could report the location of Allied ships. The British destroyer *Janus* was the first to be destroyed by a glider bomb, and by the time the Anzio beachhead was relieved the British had lost two cruisers and three destroyers to bombs and mines. US losses were somewhat less in terms of ships but more in terms of troop casualties.

The costly Anzio beachhead was not relieved until the Allied armies advanced past it toward Rome. The Allied strategy was to continue the northward advance bit by bit until the Po Valley was reached, in the wider north of Italy. After that, it was thought, the going would be easier and it might be possible to penetrate through Yugoslavia into central Europe, thereby achieving the aim of drawing as many German divisions into the south as possible.

The Allied commander-in-chief in Italy, General Harold Alexander, was one of the most competent and considerate British generals. He was sympathetic to Churchill's strategy, but was well aware that he commanded forces that were half American, not to speak of a French corps and the Poles who were to fight so triumphantly for Cassino. His plan for ending the near-stalemate at Kesselring's Gustav Line was to take the pressure off the east side and deploy most of the British Eighth Army in the center instead.

One British and one Canadian corps were to force the Rapido River and with an extensive use of smokescreens overcome the German defenses in the river valley. Artillery was to play a leading role in this attack, and in the period from May 12 to 18, about a million shells were fired, including 135,000 smoke rounds. The artillery was then to be switched to the Monte Cassino area, where two Polish divisions, dismounted cavalry for the most part, were to finally expel the Germans from the commanding heights.

Farther to the west the French Corps, which had experience of mountain warfare, was to attack other heights. Then, closer to the west coast, the US Army's II Corps would also attack. At an appropriate moment the six Allied divisions waiting at Anzio would break out and cut the main German supply and withdrawal route. This, Alexander believed, would trap the German divisions as they withdrew from the Gustav Line.

The Allied air forces were to give what support they could. An improved system of direct communications between ground units and the aircraft overhead was expected to bring good results, especially as the terrain made air support a retail rather than a wholesale operation.

The Germans had 18 divisions in this battle; 10 guarding the Gustav Line and eight besieging the Allied Anzio beachhead. The Allies had six divisions at Anzio and 11 more attacking the western part of the Gustav Line. Thus it was one of the biggest battles of the war although, as its climax coincided with the Normandy landings, it attracted relatively little public attention. The main threat to Alexander's plan was the stubborn German resistance in the Cassino area. Capturing those heights, defended mainly by German paratroops, cost the Poles 4000 casualties. But, at the expense of those casualties, the obliteration of the venerable Cassino monastery, and the virtual reshaping of the landscape, Cassino was won.

Nearby, the success of the British and US advances was considerably helped by an unexpected triumph by the French. General Alphonse Juin's French North African units, largely native soldiers, had been allocated the central mountainous sector mainly because something was needed to keep the Germans occupied in that sector. But, skilfully exploiting the lie of the land, these French units infiltrated their way toward a commanding height, captured it, and then with that advantage broke through the Gustav Line at several points. This caused a general collapse of the German defenses which up to that point had been successfully keeping the Canadian and British attackers at a distance.

The early collapse of the German defense at this, the western end, came as much as a surprise to the Allies as to the Germans. There was therefore an initial hesitation on the Allies' part, which gave the Germans time to organize a very competent and stubborn rearguard action. They retired to their next position, which Kesselring had surveyed long before and half prepared. This was the Gothic Line, crossing Italy near Florence. Alexander's aim of cutting off the retreating Germans would have been achieved had not General Clark decided to disregard orders and take most of his Fifth Army into Rome instead of eastward to cut off the Germans.

Why Clark did this has been, and may remain, a matter of controversy, although historians, with the passage of time, tend more and more to conclude that, while Clark may possibly have persuaded himself that this was tactically the best thing to do, it was nevertheless an inexcusable act of indisci-

Above: General Mark Clark's moment of triumph, or (according to taste) his fall from grace, as he surveys Rome, taken by his Fifth Army in defiance of orders to concentrate on pursuing the retreating Germans.

Above: French colonial troops made a big contribution in the Italian campaign. Here, they are shown on the march toward Sienna, which they captured in July 1944.

Left: A British Eighth Army Sherman tank passes a knocked-out German Panther during the initially successful drive of July 1944.

Above: A British Churchill tank is serviced during the Italian campaign, July 1944.

Above right: An Italian partisan, one of many who increasingly harried the German forces.

Far right: Next to his car, decorated with US, British and Polish flags, the Allied Supreme Commander, Mediterranean, General Maitland Wilson, discusses plans with the Eighth Army commander.

pline which blunted the Allied victory. Rome had little strategic significance at the time, and although the US entry into Rome might have made the Fifth Army, the US public, and Clark himself feel good, this was hardly an adequate excuse for his behavior.

The situation was delicate, and it is likely that Clark knowingly took advantage of this delicacy, which derived from the circumstances that he was an American receiving orders from a British general. But the latter was one of the most tactful of men, who had shown awareness of US sensibilities, and who moreover was in the act of successfully carrying out a well-conceived and very large operation. In the end, as Clark had no doubt calculated, no action was taken against him. On the other hand, his triumphal entry into Rome was badly upstaged by the Normandy landings, which happened the day after.

Clark's change of course, and the breakthrough itself, disorganized the Allied formations, but within days Alexander was pushing against Kesselring's rearguards. At this time the Germans had slightly more men in Italy than the Allies but it was not this, rather the terrain and the skilful German tactics, which balanced the Allied tank and air superiority. The German engineers, in particular, performed well. All bridges were blown at just the right moment, and apart from the usual hidden mines, there was a great variety of booby-traps, so that on entering towns Allied soldiers were liable to blow themselves up while doing the most ordinary things: picking a bunch of grapes, flushing a toilet and opening a door. These tactics caused relatively few casualties, but made the Allied advance very slow, since each push was necessarily followed by a period of makesafe.

Eventually the Allies pushed close to Kesselring's Gothic Line. This stretched across Italy north of Florence, from Pesaro on the east coast to La Spezia on the west. Here the Apennine range runs diagonally across the

leg of Italy, almost from coast to coast, and these mountains were the basis on which Kesselring's sappers built the Line. Any attempt to break it at its eastern end required the crossing of seven rivers, with another 12 waiting should the attack be successful and continue into the Po Valley. In the center, there were just two mountain passes, and these were heavily fortified. In the west, a breakthrough might be successful on the coastal strip but, not breaching the mountains, would merely have required the Germans to adjust their line.

The Allied plan, which was put into action in late August, was for the British Eighth Army to attack strongly up the Adriatic coast, with the main break to be attempted in the foothills about 10 miles inland. A breakthrough here would allow British tanks to penetrate behind the Gothic Line. Once this success had caused Kesselring to despatch reserves east, the US Fifth Army was to attack the two central passes.

At first, all went well. The Eighth Army, which included Canadian, Indian and Polish formations, had a bitter, close fight in which the several days of battle consisted of innumerable infantry engagements at company and platoon level for the possession of carefully-prepared strongpoints. Despite quite high casualties, the British gradually pushed back the Germans and on September 10, two weeks after the start of the attack in the east, the US Fifth Army began its own attacks on the fortified central passes.

Here again, the battle was a series of small, often heroic, actions in which the Americans slowly gained ground. But in the end Kesselring won, because the Allies exhausted their reserves. The hoped-for tank breakthrough came to nothing, largely because the British tanks were confronted once again with German 88mm antitank guns. Advancing about 30 miles, the British lost about 200 tanks. The seasonal rains began, and this made progress even more difficult.

In the center the Fifth Army for a few hours looked poised to make the vital breakthrough that would take it to Bologna. Kesselring, apparently, believed at this point that all was lost, but he was saved by bad weather that deprived the Americans of most of their air support.

With this effort, the Allied forces in Italy, already weakened by diversion of resources to the campaign in northern France, had come to the end of their strength. They had fought a great fight almost to the top of Italy's leg, but they would have to wait until April 1945 before penetrating the Gothic Line.

THE DRIVE ON GERMANY

Right: Riding a bulldozer tank, US troops pass the Siegfried Line on August 15, 1944.

Top: Dutch civilians celebrate the liberation of Eindhoven.

Above: Hitler shows Mussolini the damage caused by the attempt on his life.

Above right: The Allied broad-front strategy presses on the German western frontier.

Far right: De Gaulle and his supporters parade through liberated Paris.

By the end of August the German position in France was clearly untenable. Attempts to hold the line of the Seine only resulted in the cutting off and surrender of thousands of men and their weapons. Since the Normandy landings the German army had lost almost 250,000 men, not to speak of about 1500 tanks. Despite their aircraft shortage, the Germans also contrived to lose about 2000 planes in this campaign. The German commander, Kluge, was dismissed and like Rommel subsequently agreed to poison himself after being accused of having previous knowledge of the July Bomb Plot against Hitler. He was replaced by Model, a tough and competent character who, however, found the cards stacked against him.

There had been some changes in the Allied command, too. For the Normandy campaign Montgomery had been in charge of all the armies, British and US, with Eisenhower remaining in England as Supreme Commander. With Normandy won, Eisenhower came to take command of all the armies, displacing Montgomery. Although Montgomery was simultaneously elevated to field marshal, this concession to his vanity did not lessen his mortification at what he considered to be a demotion. But he had been given the next-best job, command of the

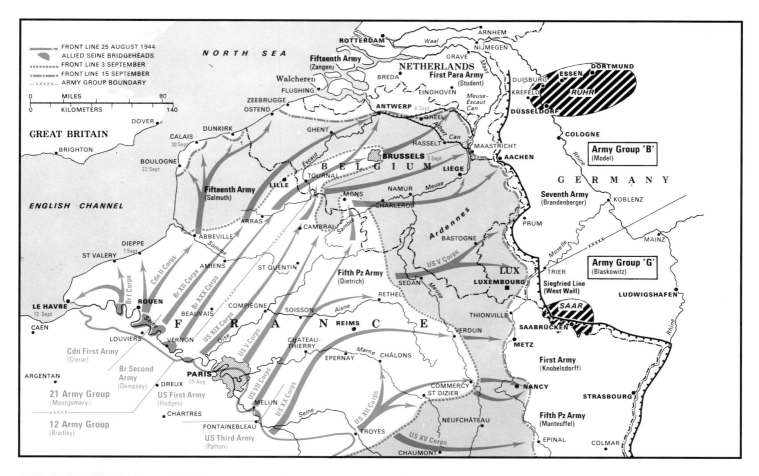

Map legend:
- FRONT LINE 25 AUGUST 1944
- ALLIED SEINE BRIDGEHEADS
- FRONT LINE 3 SEPTEMBER
- FRONT LINE 15 SEPTEMBER
- XXXXX ARMY GROUP BOUNDARY

MILES 0 — 80
KILOMETERS 0 — 140

Anglo-Canadian 21st Army Group which, because of its northerly location, was the most important of the army groups. Later, Montgomery complained that Eisenhower, back in the rear at Supreme Headquarters, could have only a poor view of the real situation, and suggested that an on-the-spot army commander-in-chief be appointed. As it was fairly plain that Montgomery envisaged this job for himself, the idea made little headway but created one more debate by which Eisenhower and his leading generals were distracted from their main concern.

Paris had fallen, although the final assault was entrusted to Leclerc's French 2nd Armored Division, not to Patton's men who had done most of the fighting but by-passed Paris. Hitler in one of his fits of petulance had ordered Paris to be burned to the ground, but his local commandant and commander both turned a blind eye to this instruction. In Paris, as elsewhere in France, the picture was confused as civilians rejoiced in the streets while many German strongpoints were still unsubdued.

The Resistance, grandly called the French Forces of the Interior, was engaged in all kinds of guerrilla and direct assaults upon German troops and supplies in France. In the meantime, Frenchmen began to slaughter

Frenchmen; accusations of collaborating with the Germans enabled many old scores to be settled by quick, no-questions-asked, rough justice. Among the dead were several patriotic Frenchmen who had wormed their way into German confidence during the occupation so convincingly that they were immediately executed as collaborators. It would be several years before some of these men and women would be posthumously rehabilitated. On a more mundane level in this confused period, any Frenchwoman who had been seen kissing a German, or who could plausibly be accused of doing so, was in peril of public humiliation, if not worse.

While in the liberated zones many of those who had lain low in the occupation came to pass themselves off as Resistance heroes, the real heroes were still at work. Among these were those French fighting men who had rallied to de Gaulle in 1940, although these were outnumbered by those who had joined his ranks since the African invasion of 1942. Also included in this select category were those of the Resistance still working at great

peril in German strongpoints, notably in the northern French ports.

Realizing how important the ports were to the Allied armies, the German command had left strong garrisons inside them. Toulon and Marseilles had been lost, but the northwestern ports of St. Nazaire, Brest and elsewhere were still closed to Allied shipping because the German garrisons were conducting very stubborn defenses. The German command well understood that with the collapse of their army in France the main brake on the Allied advance would be supply shortage.

Having so successfully put the French railroad network out of commission, the Allies by August were suffering from the inability to use rail transport, so much more efficient than highway when big tonnages were involved. Later, Eisenhower would be blamed for not exploiting German disarray by plunging forward into Germany immediately, but he simply could not do this. Cherbourg and Le Havre were still not available; Cherbourg had been captured as early as June, but had been so thoroughly wrecked that it was out of

Right: Self-propelled guns of the French 2nd Armored Division are used as cover by Parisians as they come under sniper fire, August 1944.

Below: Parisians welcome their US liberators.

Below right: Rough justice for a Frenchwoman accused of collaborating with the Germans. These primitive inquisitions were organized in good conscience by the Resistance and probably in most cases produced just verdicts even though sentences were often savage.

action for months. So supplies still came through the Mulberry harbor. That is, they were still delivered over the beach. Motor trucks took them forward, but the trucks themselves carried quite small tonnages in relation to their fuel consumption, especially after the supply lines lengthened.

An armored division was reckoned to need 900 tons of supplies daily. This included fuel, which also had to be taken by highway. By the end of August Eisenhower had in northern France the equivalent of 15 armored divisions as well as 23 infantry divisions (each of which required about 400 daily tons); this implied a daily supply demand for the equivalent of about 60 European-size freight trains, but it was to be many months before the railroads were restored, by which time the field of battle was no longer France.

At that time, late August, effective German air strength was down to three figures, whereas the Allies had about 14,000 aircraft available. In tanks, the Allies had a 20-to-one superiority. The old "Siegfried Line," or *Westwall*, built before the war to guard Ger-

many's western frontier, was largely dismantled, with most of its guns having been despatched to other fronts long before. This shaky German situation suggested to some generals, notably Montgomery (who had Churchill's support), that the war could be ended that year if a single determined thrust was made into Germany. The debate was quite acrimonious, largely because vanity as well as military effectiveness was involved. Although Eisenhower, secure in his pre-eminence, was not concerned with cutting a figure, several of the US generals, but especially the British Montgomery, had difficulty in putting aside, for the general good, questions of their personal image.

Although the Normandy landings had been meticulously planned, this was not the case with operations during the ensuing months. Rightly or wrongly, it was thought that the flow of events was so unpredictable that laying down medium-term plans was unwise. This meant, however, that certain basic issues had never been properly thrashed out in peaceful circumstances. Now, with the battle in progress, Eisenhower was subjected to different views, often uncompromisingly expressed, on what to do next in the battle.

That the Normandy campaign had been so successful was part of the problem. It had never been envisaged that Germany would be on the run so early. Eisenhower had expected the ensuing campaign to be pursued on a broad front, enabling all Allied forces to have their own go at the enemy. The possibility of a lightning, war-finishing thrust had never been thoroughly discussed. Eisenhower preferred to stick to his original plan, which was certainly less risky. Moreover, he could point to the impossibility of supplying advanced armies with all they needed. Montgomery's suggestion was that just one army should be used, with most supplies channeled to it. The fact that "just one army" was Montgomery's army did not help to persuade Eisenhower.

Montgomery was abrasive, obstinate, and

Main picture: US tank landing ships, having fulfilled their task of supporting the operations against Brest in western France, rest high and dry on a Britanny beach.

Far left: British tanks enjoy a warm welcome from the Belgians as they enter Brussels.

Left: At a time of friction, Eisenhower spends a few pleasant moments with his subordinate and old friend Patton (left).

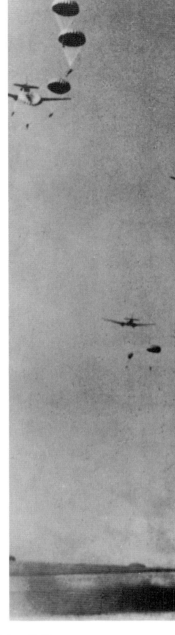

had the kind of vanity that knew how to inspire respect and devotion among his soldiers. As such, he had been an ideal commander in the hard days of the North African campaign. Later, when he had to cooperate with Americans, less familiar with his kind of character, it was clear that he was in no sense a team player. But postwar revelations by German generals indicate that Montgomery was technically right in his suggestion for an immediate thrust by his army, despite the supply problems. The Germans were perilously off-balance in August. The Bomb Plot against Hitler had removed some generals and distracted others, the losses of the Normandy campaign were hard to make up, especially in view of Russian assaults on the Eastern Front, and the German soldiers' morale, while standing up well, was certainly not at its peak.

But Eisenhower, quite apart from his preference for the plan he had already mentally adopted, would have had great difficulty in accepting Montgomery's urging. Even if supplies could be stretched, there was no margin for bad luck or for the unexpected in the proposal for a quick thrust. Since Montgomery's proposal was never put into practice, it is all too easy to say that it would have been decisive, because historians cannot know what effect ill luck, or mistakes, or surprises might have had.

There was also public opinion to be taken into account. The US press, only part of which was favorably inclined toward Britain, had already fulminated against Montgomery in June and July, when it claimed (wrongly) that he was letting the Americans do all the fighting as the Allies extended their beachheads. The idea of letting this British general execute a war-winning stroke, while the US armies looked on from a distance, was politically unacceptable.

So in the end Eisenhower did not change his mind, to the relief of Patton. Bradley, also suspicious of Montgomery, was nevertheless inclined toward the single thrust concept, but thought that Montgomery was not the best general to take charge of this. Eisenhower, because he was tactful, did not wish to antagonize the British and, because it seemed the best policy, still gave Montgomery's 21st Army Group some priority in supplies. As this army group occupied the northern sector of the front it was well poised to seize what the Allied forces most needed, a big port. Le Havre, in quite a bad state, was taken by the British in mid-September and the cross-Channel (and therefore small) ports of Boulogne and Calais would follow, but Mont-

gomery had within reach one of the world's greatest ports, Antwerp, and Antwerp lay virtually on Germany's doorstep.

At the end of August the Allied armies had advanced into Belgium from the line of the Seine. In the north, Montgomery had Canada's First Army and the British Second Army. To his south Bradley's 12th Army Group included the US First Army and Patton's Third Army. Meanwhile from the south of France the 6th Army Group (US Seventh and French First Armies) had rounded Switzerland and turned east to threaten Alsace and southwestern Germany. The drive along the Channel coast by the Canadian First Army was especially necessary, because it overran the launching sites that had just begun to bombard London with destructive V-1 flying bombs. The British Second Army meanwhile was making fast progress toward Brussels, while Patton was at the French fortress town of Verdun.

Even without accepting Montgomery's concept of a knock-out blow, the Allied forces should have done better in September. Possibly because they were so distracted by internal arguments, they let slip several opportunities. One of these was failure to maintain pressure against the Germans. Soon the magic moment had passed when the German armies seemed helpless. In late September all Germans, and not just the army, were morally strengthened when Churchill and Roosevelt backed the so-called Morgenthau Plan, which not only demanded unconditional surrender, but also visualized the razing of German industrial cities and the call-up

Above: The US 82nd Airborne Division makes a drop near Nijmegen during Operation Market Garden.

Far left: Having served its purpose, a US troop-carrying glider lies abandoned in the Market Garden operation.

Left: British airborne troops destined for the Arnhem operation wait to board their gliders, one of which can be seen (left) beyond the row of tugs.

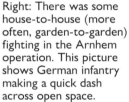

Left: British paratroopers take cover in a shellhole during the battle for Arnhem.

Right: There was some house-to-house (more often, garden-to-garden) fighting in the Arnhem operation. This picture shows German infantry making a quick dash across open space.

Above: The famous bridge too far – the Arnhem road bridge photographed just as the operation ended. At its northern end is a column of wrecked German armored vehicles that had hurried across the bridge, only to be assailed by British paratroopers when it reached the other side.

of German workers to serve under what were virtually slave labor conditions. With this on the Allied menu, Germans preferred to fight on to the end.

Under Model, the German army pulled itself together very quickly; the crossing of the Rhine, so militarily and psychologically vital for the Allies, was likely to prove a long process. As Churchill well knew, this delay was specially damaging for Britain, for whom 1944 was very much the end of the road. By that year her foreign exchange was gone, and all possible ways of increasing the industrial labor force and the forces had been exhausted. Henceforth, despite the will for victory, her contribution would inevitably decline.

Another opportunity was lost at Antwerp in early September. Montgomery captured this big port in good condition, but the Allied planners seem to have given no consideration to what to do next. Thanks to the delay in deciding what to do, the Germans strengthened their positions along the Scheldt, the river leading to Antwerp from the sea. So the Allies at last possessed a fine port, but could not use it.

Although the time was long past when a quick blow could have finished the Germans, Montgomery's enthusiasm was undimmed, and Eisenhower, unconvinced but exhausted perhaps by Montgomery's persistent argument, raised no serious objections to the proposal to capture vital crossings over the Rhine and its tributaries in Holland. Possession of such crossings would enable the Allies to pour into Germany's industrial heartland, the Ruhr. Another argument was that airborne forces were available in Britain, and had nothing to do. The big argument against the operation, apart from the uncertainty of its success, was that it diverted resources (and minds) from the far more important, if less exciting, task of opening the Scheldt.

Known originally as Market Garden, the operation is usually referred to by its key battle, Arnhem. At the time, Montgomery was only 70 miles from Arnhem, but the Germans could be expected to put up strong resistance and then, when they had retreated

across the Rhine, blow the vital bridges. Montgomery's scheme was to send paratroops to three drop areas, from which they could capture bridges over two tributaries at Grave and Nijmegen, and over the Rhine at Arnhem, the northernmost of the drops. Having secured the bridges from demolition, the paratroops would then hang on until relieved by the British XXX Corps, fighting its way up the road northward out of Belgium.

With luck and good management, the operation might have succeeded, but it had neither. The bad management consisted in the unwillingness to change plans in the face of the unexpected. Indeed, it might be argued that there was enough last-minute intelligence information to justify a total abandonment of the plan. Among this information was the discovery that Arnhem was the place where two panzer divisions had been sent for rest and reorganization; proponents of the operation argued that if these battle-hardened German formations were resting they were unlikely to take effective action until it was too late. Dutch officers pointed out that the roads were built on embankments over the flat polders; the relieving

tanks would therefore be sitting targets as they advanced northward.

The two US airborne divisions did quite well, ensconcing themselves in the two southerly drop zones. The British airborne division scheduled to take Arnhem was less fortunate. The paratroops and the glider troops landed no less than eight miles from the bridge they were supposed to capture in a lighting swoop. The equipment they carried was enough to slow their progress but of no use against the successive, hastily-formed, lines of panzer troops with their guns and armored vehicles. More equipment for the paratroopers was available, but because there were not enough aircraft, these deliveries had been scheduled to take place over two-three days, which was plainly inadequate. In the circumstances, the advance of one British battalion to capture and hold the Arnhem road bridge was a stirring achievement; the railroad bridge had already been blown.

Meanwhile a dead American officer, found by the Germans in a crashed glider, was discovered to be carrying complete plans for the operation. With this, the Germans could anti-

cipate further Allied moves and one of their first priorities was to move anti-aircraft weapons to the areas that they now knew would be used for further Allied drops. The British cup of misfortune was filled when the paratroopers discovered that their radios did not work, so, whereas the Germans could communicate by radio or over the civilian telephone system, the British commanders were usually out of touch with their units during the confused fighting.

Bad weather was genuine bad luck for which, however, allowance should have been made. This prevented the exploitation of Allied air power to recover from the initial misfortunes. On September 22 the land forces arriving from the south did relieve the US airborne troops at the Nijmegen bridge, bringing that crossing of the River Waal into permanent Allied control, but Arnhem could not be relieved. Here the outnumbered and besieged British fought one of the closest and hardest engagements of the war, winning five Victoria Crosses in the process, but the enormous press publicity devoted to their courage only obscured (as was intended) the reality of a costly fiasco drawing to a close.

CLOSING IN
ON JAPAN

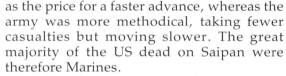

Previous pages: Some of the hundreds of ships involved in the Leyte landings.

Above: The triple 16-inch turrets of the new battleship USS *Iowa* open fire on Tinian.

Below: A Japanese airfield on Tinian is ravaged by US carrier aircraft.

The end of the fighting on Saipan left both sides needing to re-think their tactics. For the Japanese, the question of how strong the shoreline defense should be once more demanded attention. For the Americans, there had been a point where the different tactics of the Marines and the US Army had been blatantly obvious and gave rise to some bitterness. This happened when the army division on the island was flanked by the two Marine divisions; in the advance this line soon became concave as the army units lagged behind. The reason for this was simply that the Marines habitually fought with more dash, accepting higher casualties as the price for a faster advance, whereas the army was more methodical, taking fewer casualties but moving slower. The great majority of the US dead on Saipan were therefore Marines.

Neither the Japanese nor the Americans quite solved their problems. Indeed, the first response of the American command, replacement of the army division's commander, simply concealed the dilemma. In later battles the Americans found ways to alleviate their problem, while by the end of the war Japanese island defenders had largely abandoned the concept of shoreline defense.

After Saipan, the next target in the Marianas was Guam. First landings were by Marines on each side of the Orote peninsula. Fighting with great determination, the Japanese were slowly pushed back and almost 2000 Americans were killed before the island was taken. Over 17,000 of the defenders died, and a few took to the wilds, with one only emerging in 1972.

On the third of the main islands, Tinian, the Japanese had about 4700 soldiers and 4100 naval guards. On this occasion the Marines' tactics were different, with a feint landing threatening Tinian town in the south while the real landings took place on two small beaches in the north. The division offering the feint attack then joined the main landing. As usual, the Japanese made a noisy but ineffective counterattack on the beaches during the night but were then gradually pushed into the southeast tip of the island, where they put up their last fight on August 1. Two weeks previously, discredited by the events in the Marianas and the naval defeat, General Tojo's government had been replaced by another which, however, was still dominated by the army.

When the airfields of these three islands were taken it was no longer a question of simply moving in US fighters and fighter-bombers. The intention was to rebuild them with better runways, and more workshops and stores, so that they could become bases for B-29 heavy bombers. In October the first B-29s took off for a raid on Truk, and soon they were reaching the Japanese mainland.

With Japan in effective range, the question of strategy could no longer be postponed. MacArthur wanted to aim at the Philippines which, once recaptured, could be used as the base for a final assault on Japan itself. The navy preferred its central Pacific strategy, which would by-pass the Philippines and invade Formosa instead, from where it would be easy to set up bases for a final assault on

Japan; such bases might be on the Chinese coast or in the Ryukyu Islands.

MacArthur was strongly influenced by emotional attachment to the Philippines, but his plan did have advantages. To leave the pro-American Filipinos under Japanese control until the end of the war, argued MacArthur, would be disloyal if not disreputable. Moreover, as the Filipino population was friendly it would be a surer foundation for an American base than the Formosans, who were Japan-oriented. In the end, President Roosevelt chose MacArthur's proposal, and this was confirmed at the Quebec Conference in September.

This conference also adopted a timetable. MacArthur and the Pacific fleet would jointly stage a landing at Leyte, in the Philippines, in December. As a preliminary, some of the intervening islands would be taken, either to eliminate Japanese airfields or to provide bases for the Americans. At the time of the conference Admiral William F. Halsey with his Third Fleet was seeking targets on the

Below: President Roosevelt comes to Hawaii in July 1944 to decide strategy. Admiral Nimitz (with pointer) advocated an island-to-island approach to Japan across the central Pacific while General MacArthur (left) preferred an advance through the Philippines.

islands scheduled for invasion, but met with surprisingly little opposition. Halsey therefore continued to the Philippines where, again, he obtained only a small response from the Japanese.

He concluded that the Japanese were very weak, and therefore the December schedule for invading the Philippines was decidedly pessimistic. He shared his thoughts with his commander-in-chief Nimitz, and the latter contacted the Joint Chiefs of Staff who were still conferring in Quebec. It was thereupon decided that the Leyte operation should be advanced by two months. This gave little time for planning, but MacArthur's staff had already shown its high competence and in fact this new deadline presented few planning problems.

The new schedule meant that some of the previously planned landings, at the island of Yap and at a bay on the Philippines' southernmost island, Mindanao, were no longer necessary. However, other islands were already being fought over. After Morotai was captured against slight opposition, American and Australian constructional troops moved in to prepare an airfield that could be used as a staging post for medium-size aircraft on their way to Leyte. A base at Morotai also neutralized the several Japanese airfields on the nearby island of Halmahera. The Japanese command fully realized the significance of Morotai, put its planners to work, but concluded that without air power Morotai could not be recaptured.

Another island, Peleliu, was attacked mainly because the invasion force was already on its way when second thoughts began to be expressed about its value. Probably it would have been better to have bypassed it, because it was strongly defended by more than 5000 Japanese, who were well entrenched in depth, having dug intricate and deep caves into the soft coral rock. In the end, only flame-throwers could dislodge the enemy from those caves. The landings took place on September 15, but the Japanese held out until November 24, and almost 2000 American lives were spent in this prolonged struggle.

Much more useful was Ulithi atoll, easily taken on September 23 and providing a fleet-size anchorage. Task Force 38, or Fast Carrier Forces, was there at the beginning of October, but soon left for one of the more important preliminaries of the Leyte landing, the neutralization of Formosa. Lying between Japan and the northern Philippines, Formosa was an important base for the Japanese, as well as a staging post, and TF

38's main task was to destroy whatever air power was based there, and to wreck the airfields. How much strength the Japanese would muster was uncertain and TF 38's nine large and eight light carriers, with attendant battleships and other vessels, was not too large, given the scale and the uncertainties of its task.

Before tackling Formosa TF 38 attacked airfields on Okinawa, lying between Formosa and Japan. In the Formosa operation, luck, in the form of three days of good flying weather, favored the Americans. The first sweep, as dawn was breaking, was by fighters. These were intended to gain immediate command of the air, and largely succeeded. Fighter-bombers followed, and in the course of those three days over 2000 sorties were made. The Japanese were not passive, however, and their aircraft succeeded in damaging two cruisers and a carrier. B-29 bombers from Chinese bases also joined in on the final day, and the final tally of the American onslaught was over 500 enemy planes destroyed, plus dozens of freighters as well as dumps and barracks.

The navy's loss was 79 aircraft; this was a bearable price, especially as many of the Japanese aircraft destroyed had been intended as replacements for the Japanese navy's losses in the Battle of the Philippine Sea. This finally sealed the fate of the Japanese navy's air arm, and in the final big

Main picture: Tank landing ships at Leyte. These particular units were Coastguard-manned.

Above: General Douglas MacArthur returns to the Philippines, accompanied (extreme left) by the President of the Philippines.

Top: One of the Japanese attackers of USS *Princeton* hits the water, while a sister carrier makes an evasive turn.

Above: The Japanese battleship *Musashi* lives her last minutes as she comes under air attack in the Sibuyan Sea during the Leyte naval battles.

to secure its own fuel supplies. Soon afterward, on the basis of the reported victory, imperial headquarters abandoned its original plan of holding everything in reserve for a decisive battle on the biggest Philippine island, Luzon. Believing that US carrier strength, and hence US local air power, had been decimated, it decided to transfer the "decisive battle" to Leyte as soon as it realized the Americans were landing there.

By this stage of the war Japanese staff work was obviously suffering from both lack of zest and inflexibility. This had been true ever since the Japanese offensive petered out in 1942, when defense took on more significance. It might have been expected that by 1944 some adaptation to circumstances would have been achieved, but in fact ineptitude still prevailed in the high command.

Only two responses to the American advances could be envisaged. There was the policy of "protracted action," which really meant holding out for as long as possible while inflicting as many casualties as possible, and there was the "decisive action." The latter had long been a feature of Japanese doctrine, and the first months of the war seemed to confirm its validity, but by 1944 it was little more than blind faith in a big battle in which, somehow, Japanese forces would win a crushing victory. Repeatedly, the Japanese command planned for this decisive action, confidently expecting the Americans to act as it expected them to act.

The Allies had fixed October 20 for the Leyte landings, and in early October MacArthur, who had the Seventh Fleet under his command as well, began to concentrate his ships at harbors along the northern coast of New Guinea. He had 738 vessels in total, a little less than the total of the Normandy landings but the scale of the operation, in terms of distances between base and beach, was much greater.

Preceded by minesweepers, the armada set off on October 10 and on the 17th the minesweepers were clearing passages between the small islands that dotted the entry to Leyte Gulf. The islands were at the same time occupied by Rangers, and on the 19th the bombarding battleships and cruisers were able to steam into the Gulf and begin their work of clearing the beaches of any enemy who might be there. Further devastation was wreaked by aircraft from the 16 small escort carriers of MacArthur's Seventh Fleet.

The bombardment was hardly needed, for the beaches were virtually undefended. Two beaches, Tacloban and Dulag, had been chosen, 10 miles distant from each other, and

naval battle the Japanese would have to fight without effective air cover.

The Japanese completely misinterpreted the result of the Formosan engagements. At first, the official Tokyo claim that the Americans had lost 11 carriers and two battleships was regarded in western circles as simply an inept propaganda effort, but in fact this is what the Japanese command believed. It had made the cardinal error of accepting uncritically the reports of its aviators. The latter, having seen from different angles the hits on US ships, overestimated the actual hits and, moreover, tended to identify cruisers as battleships and small aircraft carriers as fleet aircraft carriers.

The Japanese navy was so pleased with itself that it proposed a pursuit of the supposedly crippled American task force, but the army objected, largely because for such an offensive the navy would need scarce tankers, and the army wanted to keep them

with the fine weather, and absence of mines and underwater obstacles, the landings could proceed according to plan. A new type of large landing ship was at the disposal of the Americans. This was the 900-ton LSM (Landing Ship Medium), which was faster than the older LCT but provided equal vehicle capacity. As was characteristic of US amphibious landings, enormous strength was landed in the very first stages; by October 21 over 132,000 men were already ashore, with 200,000 tons of supplies. On the 22nd, MacArthur himself strolled ashore, accompanied by the Filipino president.

To defend the whole of the Philippines the Japanese General Yamashita had an army of 350,000 men, but he had only been able to allocate 16,000 men to Leyte. Both Yamashita and his second-in-command had only recently been appointed to the Philippines; in fact, the second-in-command landed the same day as the Americans. This unfamiliarity with local circumstances was a severe handicap, and was another example of the lack of imagination prevailing in the Japanese high command.

Another handicap, by no means new but perhaps more damaging in days of defeat, was the inability of the army and navy commands to work harmoniously together, and there was also friction between different levels of the army command. In November, when the Philippine campaign was at its most critical point, a longstanding argument about where the Japanese Southern Army's HQ should be located came to a head when that HQ left the Philippines and installed itself in faraway Saigon.

The Americans were pressing ahead quickly, knowing that the faster they moved the less chance the Japanese would have to build those in-depth defenses at which they excelled. Also, they expected that Yamashita would try to send reinforcements from the other islands. So fast was the progress of these US Army formations that both Dulag and Tacloban airfields fell into their hands on October 21. Tacloban was also valuable because it possessed the only docks on the island. By that time the Gulf itself was without navy ships, but there remained about 30 freighters waiting to unload.

In the following weeks the fighting on Leyte became tougher. Before the last sea

Above: A few yards from the beach, US troops of the 1st Cavalry Division cautiously move inland after the Leyte landing. The smoke and flames come from a fuel dump ignited by naval bombardment. By this stage of the war (October 1944) the invasion troops were quite familiar with this kind of terrain.

approach to the island was sealed off the Japanese had managed to bring in 45,000 more men, and much of the territory ahead of the Americans was mountainous. One US corps tried to capture the mountains commanding the Japanese supply base at Ormoc but was held back by a stubborn defense. Ormoc did not fall until December, when a US division was landed to the south, thereby outflanking it. The US forces at Ormoc then fought their way to the north, where they met the oncoming troops that had originally landed at Tacloban. After December 25 the Japanese were no longer able to put up organized resistance, but here and there small pockets conducted their own defense, and some of these were not quelled until 1945.

Before the fighting subsided in Leyte, other parts of the Philippines were assaulted. Samar, Leyte's close neighbor to the north, was soon secured. The island of Mindoro, essential as a stepping-stone toward the biggest island, Luzon, was invaded in December, in full knowledge that it might be a tough assignment. Soon after setting out, the invasion convoy was attacked by suicide planes. One of these put a destroyer out of action and another, more selective, succeeded in crashing into the cruiser *Nashville*, killing many of the staff officers directing the invasion. Despite this setback, the landings took place as planned, without immediate shoreline opposition; there were few Japanese troops on the island, and a landing had not been expected at that point.

Although the Mindoro landing had been easy, supplying the troops was a problem. Japanese suicide aircraft soon sank five freighters and five LSTs. Around Christmas the army's P-38 aircraft were operating from a local airfield, which brought some improvement, but the remnants of the Japanese navy, including two cruisers, were trying to break through to Mindoro. Army air force planes, mainly fighters, were sent to the reported position of the Japanese ships while the only other available naval support, PT motor torpedo boats, also went out. With these American diversionary tactics the shore bombardment made by the Japanese was mainly ineffective and, after losing a destroyer to a PT-boat, the Japanese retired. After this, Mindoro was soon captured. The next step would be to Luzon, in January.

In the meantime the last big naval battle of the war had been fought. Not only was the Battle of Leyte Gulf the final large engagement, but it was also the last battle of the dreadnought era, for there would be no more gunnery contests between battleships. The short fight between US and Japanese battleships was only part of this wide-ranging battle, and would probably have not taken place at all if the Japanese navy had been able to muster effective air strength. In surface ships as well as aircraft, the Japanese were outnumbered, with 64 units of their fleet engaged against 216 American (and three Australian) ships. The combined total of 283 ships also made Leyte the world's biggest-ever naval battle.

The encounter, once again, was a product of the Japanese quest for a "decisive battle." Expecting an American landing in the Philip-

Main picture: Photographed from his target, a Japanese Kamikaze pilot aims at the carrier *Essex*. A second later, this plane struck the carrier.

Above left: The Japanese aircraft carrier *Zuikaku*, damaged by aircraft from USS *Essex* during the Battle of the Philippine Sea.

Above right: USS *Suwanee*, an escort carrier, is struck by a Japanese Kamikaze plane at the end of the Battle of Leyte Gulf.

at Leyte. To do this the covering strength provided by the US Third Fleet's Task Force 38 was to be decoyed away to the north by a force including four aircraft carriers under Ozawa's command; those carriers would be capable of launching only feeble air strikes, but that was not their purpose.

As soon as Task Force 38 had been drawn away, Admiral Kurita's Center Force, which included the two monster-battleships *Yamato* and *Musashi*, and which had been steaming from its oiling base in British North Borneo, would emerge. Its course would take it through the Philippines from west to east and it would appear at San Bernardino Strait, north of Samar but within striking distance of Leyte to its south. On its way from Borneo it would detach some of its battleships under Admiral Nishimura to form a Southern Force that would cross the Philippine archipelago in the south and then turn north toward Leyte.

This southern force was to be reinforced en route by ships sent down from the north under Admiral Shima. Thus the Americans at Leyte would be attacked from both north and south by striking forces that included battleships, at a time when they would lack the cover of Task Force 38; only the relatively weak US Seventh Fleet, under MacArthur's command, would be off Leyte. After routing the Americans and their Seventh Fleet, the combined Japanese forces would await battle with TF 38.

With its elements of surprise and different lines of attack the plan had its strengths, but it depended on the Americans doing what they were expected to do, and the final phase, battle with Task Force 38, was a dubious proposition, given the US dominance in the air. However, on this occasion the Americans would do what they were expected to do, for Admiral Halsey would take the bait of Ozawa's northern force and leave Leyte exposed.

US submarines made a great contribution to spoiling the Japanese plan. On the one hand, they failed to spot Ozawa's decoy force, and on the other they not only spotted Kurita's movements but also sank two of his heavy cruisers and crippled another. This was not a good start for Kurita, especially as one of the sunken cruisers, *Atago*, was his flagship. He and some staff officers were transferred to another ship, but the experience may have contributed to Kurita's psychological tensions later in the battle.

The first phase of the battle was in the Sibuyan Sea. Task Force 38 was awaiting Kurita's ships but was attacked by land-

pines but not knowing which island would be chosen, the Japanese navy command had drawn up alternative plans. As soon as it was clear that the Americans were landing in the Leyte Gulf, the appropriate plan was put into effect. A swift swoop on the American ships while they were still unloading was out of the question; the Japanese units were widely dispersed because tanker shortage meant that they had to be based close to their fuel sources. This meant that it would be a week before the various Japanese squadrons could reach Leyte.

The aim of the Japanese was to bring a striking force within range of the US shipping

based Japanese bombers, which managed to hit the light carrier *Princeton*. Lacking, like other US carriers, any deck armor, the bomb went through several decks and exploded the carrier's torpedo stocks. This not only finished the carrier but seriously damaged the light cruiser *Birmingham* nearby. However, while this was going on, aircraft from another of TF 38's task groups had located Kurita's main force. Bomb and torpedo planes from five carriers were despatched and the new super-battleship *Musashi*, hit by 19 torpedoes and several bombs, went down. Other of Kurita's ships were hit, and the consequent delays meant that he would not be able to reach Leyte at the same time as the southern force, as had been planned.

The following night, 24-25 October, the southern force attempted to break into Leyte Gulf through the Surigao Strait. Its main strength was two middle-aged battleships, *Fuso* and *Yamashiro*, and three heavy cruisers. It had been sighted by US carrier planes at noon, and the commander of the US Seventh Fleet, Admiral Thomas Kinkaid, made dispositions accordingly. His six elderly battleships, originally intended for shore bombardment, were placed at the exit of Surigao Strait, supported by four heavy and four light cruisers. Destroyers and motor torpedo boats were sent down the strait to locate and harry the enemy. The MTBs, or PT-boats, were to play an essential scouting role because of the unavailability of radar-equipped patrol planes capable of night operations.

Nishimura, commanding the Southern Force, knew that he would not meet Kurita's Center Force as planned, but nevertheless pushed on, aware that without air cover his only chance of getting to Leyte was to pass the Surigao Strait in darkness. PT-boats soon picked him up, and although their successive torpedo attacks were unsuccessful, they passed on the essential information of his course and speed.

In the small hours Nishimura faced attacks by US destroyer divisions. *Fuso* was sunk by a torpedo, as were three Japanese destroyers, and *Yamashiro* received two torpedoes, but was able to continue on her way. So Nishimura's Southern Force, as it approached the head of the Surigao Strait, consisted of the damaged *Yamashiro*, the heavy cruiser *Mogami*, and a destroyer. Awaiting them were the US battleships.

Just as superior US radar had aided the preceding torpedo attacks, so did radar determine the fate of Nishimura. Three of the US battleships had modern fire-control radar but the others did not, so it was the guns of those

sure how this would be accomplished. But one fact was now in his favor. During the afternoon of October 24 Admiral Ozawa at last succeeded in getting himself noticed by Admiral Halsey's Task Force 38. Four aircraft carriers, plus two battleships converted to semi-carriers, were a powerful bait for Halsey. Ozawa had already lost most of the few aircraft he possessed in making an attack on one of Halsey's task groups. The attack had been fruitless, but was part of Ozawa's effort to attract attention.

Halsey, in an error of judgment which fortunately was not quite fatal, took all possible forces to meet Ozawa. One of his task groups had been detached for refueling, but he still had three carrier groups with almost 800 aircraft (by this time Ozawa had less than 30 planes left). He took all three carrier groups, plus the battleship group, to meet Ozawa. With 64 ships against 17, this was overkill, and Halsey, knowing that Kurita's Center Force was still in the vicinity, should have at least left his battleships close to Leyte. One reason why he did not was that, unwarily, he had taken at face value the reports of his aircrews who had attacked Kurita the previous day. As usual, these reports were over-optimistic and gave the impression that Kurita's force had been rendered ineffective.

Kurita's battleships and cruisers emerged at dawn off Samar, close to the escort carrier group that was covering Leyte. Within minutes the escort carriers, taken by surprise, were under fire. These carriers were part of the Seventh Fleet, under MacArthur's command and Halsey, of the Third Fleet, had not informed Seventh Fleet that one of his planes had seen Kurita's force approaching up the San Bernardino Strait.

So the escort carriers, carrying few attack planes and in a poor position to launch them, found themselves within range of four enemy battleships and six heavy cruisers. The carriers had only five-inch guns, like the three destroyers and four destroyer escorts that were accompanying them. There were two other escort carrier groups nearby, making a total of 16 ships carrying 235 fighters and 143 torpedo planes, but many of those planes were already away on various missions.

What should then have occurred was a slaughter of the US carriers, caught under heavy guns. That this disaster did not happen was partly because Kurita (equally surprised, and believing that the escort carriers were Halsey's fleet carriers) made fundamental mistakes, partly because Admiral Clifton A. Sprague, the carrier group's commander,

Above: USS *Suwanee* is struck by a Kamikaze aircraft at the close of the Leyte battle; the carrier was damaged, but not sunk. A second Kamikaze, pursued by a US plane, can also be seen.

Left: An escort carrier hurriedly flies off its planes as Japanese ships attack off Samar.

three, plus lighter guns from radar-equipped cruisers, that quelled *Yamashiro*. That battleship, burning brightly, was finally sent to the bottom by a destroyer's torpedoes. Nishimura went with her.

The badly damaged *Mogami* then retired back down the strait and was soon in collision with a heavy cruiser, part of Admiral Shima's reinforcement for the Southern Force. Finally aware that the Southern Force no longer existed, Shima also turned round. At dawn the pursuing US cruisers caught up with *Mogami*, but were unable to sink her before being recalled. However, Avengers flown off the escort carriers discovered her, and finally sank her.

Kurita, meanwhile, was obstinately pushing forward, still intent on devastating the US transports at Leyte but, apparently, not quite made no mistakes, and partly because enough luck and heroism were deployed to save the US vessels.

Luckily for Sprague, the wind direction was such that he could launch planes while steaming away from the approaching enemy. He deployed his carriers in a circle, with his few escorts patrolling outside the area in which the enemy shells were falling, each salvo getting closer to the carriers. Occasional rain squalls gave the Americans temporary relief, and a desperate counterattack by the escorting ships was ordered.

Kurita, meanwhile, assured by his staff that the escort carriers were fleet carriers and that the US destroyers were cruisers, made the mistake of ordering a general attack, which meant that each of his ships acted on its own initiative, uncontrolled by the flag-ship. With fierce onslaughts by those aircraft the Americans had managed to launch, plus self-sacrificial attacks by the US escorting ships, the Japanese ships became confused and let slip many opportunities. Three of the US escorts were sunk, but not before they had delayed the Japanese progress and secured a torpedo hit on one of the cruisers.

Aircraft from the other two escort carrier groups joined in, and even when ammunition was exhausted their crews made dummy attacks at the Japanese, diverting them from their main task of destroying the US carriers. Wildcat fighters attacked with machine guns.

Kurita's heavy cruisers finally pulled themselves together to make a coordinated attack on the carriers, and succeeded in sinking one of them, *Gambier Bay*. But Avengers sank two of the cruisers and at that point, when the surviving pair of Japanese cruisers had at last got themselves into a position where they could have devastated the surviving carriers, Kurita decided that enough was enough, and broke off the action. He had been ill-served by his staff, who compounded misjudgment with misinformation, and the malfunctioning Japanese radio communications did not provide a clear picture of what was happening. So, at the time Kurita called off the action, he had no idea how close he was to success. All the same, even if he had gone on to destroy the US carriers he would have been too late to catch the US transports unprepared, and would no doubt have lost more of his ships to air strikes later that day.

After Kurita retired, the escort carriers were still in action, coping with suicide planes flying from the mainland. Another carrier, *St Lo*, was sunk by one of these, and others damaged. Meanwhile Admiral Halsey's Task Force 38 was dealing with Ozawa

Below: Part of Task Force 38 at sea. Behind the two carriers, only a small part of the Task Force's air strength, come its modern 16-inch gun battleships. They are approaching Ulithi for resupply in December 1944, after the main battles of the Philippine campaign.

Bottom: *The New York Times* reports the Battle of Leyte Gulf, but also find space on its front page for domestic politics.

Right: Gunners of USS *Ommaney Bay* watch as a Japanese Kamikaze misses their escort carrier and dives into the sea. An elderly battleship, rebuilt after Pearl Harbor, is on the horizon.

The New York Times.

LATE CITY EDITION

"All the News That's Fit to Print"

VOL. XCIV..No. 31,667.

NEW YORK, THURSDAY, OCTOBER 26, 1944.

THREE CENTS NEW YORK CITY

U. S. DEFEATS JAPANESE NAVY; ALL FOE'S SHIPS IN ONE FLEET HIT; MANY SUNK; BATTLE CONTINUES

in that phase of the Leyte operations known as the Battle of Cape Engano. Halsey's scouting aircraft had at last sighted Ozawa's force before dawn on October 25, and the three carrier groups in Task Force 38 launched a first strike when it was light. Helldiver dive-bombers went in first, closely followed by low-flying fighters to divert attention from the third wave of Avenger torpedo bombers.

Without fighter cover, Ozawa did well to escape with one carrier sunk and another damaged. The second American strike, arriving soon after, caught the Japanese as they were still coping with the damage caused by the first. Another carrier was mortally injured and in the third strike the veteran carrier *Zuikaku* succumbed to three torpedoes. A fourth strike accounted for the final carrier. The aircraft-carrying battleships fared better, partly because they had far more effective anti-aircraft defense. In fact, the gunnery of the Japanese had considerably improved since the earlier years of the war. This, and Ozawa's competent handling of his decoy force, ensured that despite their overwhelming numbers the US aircraft did not gain a quick victory.

Meanwhile Halsey's modern battleships, which both his commander Nimitz and Mac-Arthur believed were still protecting Leyte, remained with him. He had received a plea for assistance against Kurita's Center Force but decided not to release the battleships, which he hoped would engage the fleeing Ozawa with their guns. In the end, feeling insulted, he complied with an order to send the battleships back, but they arrived hours after Kurita had departed.

So Ozawa's surviving ships escaped, having performed their decoy task admirably. But they had been noticed too late, and in any case Ozawa's competence had been betrayed by the mistakes of Kurita and Nishimura. Because of the air factor, the "decisive battle" off Leyte would have resulted in a Japanese defeat, but with better leadership the Japanese might have wreaked considerable loss on the Americans.

After this battle the surviving ships of the Japanese navy were clearly insufficient for their tasks. Apart from the overwhelming strength of the American fleets, pushing ever closer to Japan itself, since mid-1944 the British Far Eastern Fleet had also been applying pressure with aircraft carrier raids on ports and industries in the Dutch East Indies. Such attacks did not lead to big naval battles, but they were damaging to the Japanese war effort because they were aimed at the vital oil industry of Sumatra.

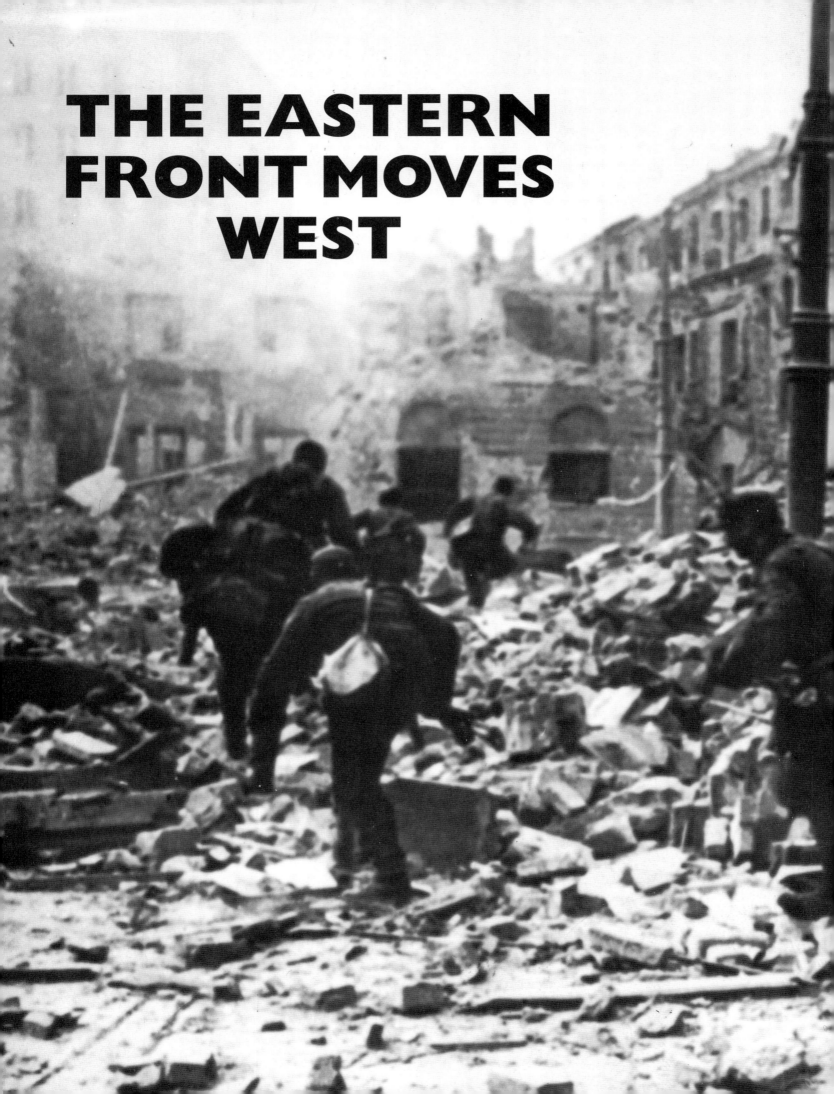

THE EASTERN
FRONT MOVES
WEST

The Red Army's winter and spring offensives had more or less cleared southern Russia of German forces and the first stage of the summer offensive was to clear central Russia and most of Belorussia, routing the German Army Group Center in the process.

Overall command was entrusted to Marshal Georgi Zhukov, who in earlier years had been directing the army at *Stavka*, and was Stalin's chief military adviser. He had supervised most of the Soviet offensives, including the Stalingrad operations, and was sometimes sent to take command of army groups at crucial times. In April 1944 General N. F. Vatutin, commander of the 1st Ukrainian Group that had made so much trouble for the Germans around Kiev, was murdered by anti-Soviet Ukrainian partisans. Sent by Stalin to replace Vatutin, Zhukov nevertheless found time to keep an eye on the offensive farther north.

Four Russian army groups, totaling about 100 divisions, took part in this massive offensive, which began in late June with an artillery barrage. The Russians were now able to mass 400 guns per mile of line, and with this crushing bombardment of its front and partisan attacks on supplies in its rear, Army Group Center found itself in peril. The Russians soon made a 250-mile gap in the German line, and sent their armor ahead of the infantry, with some air support. By this time Hitler had adopted the "hedgehog" principle of defense, which prescribed a series of mutually-supporting strongpoints, and this made it psychologically as well as tactically difficult to abandon positions.

Many formations were cut off, and Hitler ordered them to fight until relieved. This would have been sensible, if only there had been means to relieve them. As a result, virtually the whole of German Army Group Center, 25 out of 33 divisions, was destroyed. In terms of loss, this was a major disaster for the Germans; well over 500,000 men lost, with 10,000 guns and 2000 tanks and self-propelled guns. Although the numerical preponderance of the Russians was the main factor in this defeat, the generalship of Zhukov and the improved performance of Russian staff officers helped to turn the German defeat into a catastrophe.

Minsk was captured early in July, and on July 4 the Red Army crossed the old Polish frontier. The victorious Russian army groups pushed on, taking Vilnius and Grodno, thereby clearing the way to East Prussia. Meanwhile, to the south, two Ukrainian army groups were also advancing so that by August Soviet forces were close to Warsaw, although to take the city a forcing of the Vistula would have been necessary.

At this point the Polish Resistance in Warsaw, the "Polish Home Army," cast aside its conspiratorial cover and launched the Warsaw uprising. The Polish Home Army was anti-communist, and its sympathies lay with the exiled Polish government in London. The fact that the Russian armies halted outside Warsaw while the Germans suppressed this rising in a long drawn-out SS operation was ascribed to malevolence on Stalin's part. He did not want this right-wing Polish movement to succeed, it was alleged. However, it is more likely that practical considerations were responsible. The Polish Home Army had miscalculated, being in a difficult position; it wanted to take advantage of the Russian advance yet at the same time capture Warsaw itself, rather than let the Red Army do it. The rising came just as the Russian armies needed to rest and reorganize.

In fact, just as the Polish Home Army was at its last gasp in September, Stalin was envisaging an offensive to capture Warsaw, but was dissuaded by Zhukov, who saw no necessity for speed and thought the Warsaw venture would demand too many resources for too insignificant a gain. It would be January 1945 before the Red Army entered Warsaw.

In the north the German Army Group North, fallen back from Leningrad, was pushed farther back in July. It faced the prospect of being cut off by Soviet forces that were entering East Prussia, but Hitler refused permission to retreat and the Army Group therefore stayed close to the Baltic, and was cut off when Russian forces took Narva and Riga. Army Group North, still a quite valuable part of the German army, was accordingly denied any further role in the war.

The withdrawal of the Germans from Leningrad enabled the Red Army to advance against the Finns without risk of exposing its rear. Five armies were devoted to this, and they advanced up the Karelian Isthmus in June, skirting both sides of Lake Onega. The Finns fought their customary skilful retreat but soon the Mannerheim Line was broken and Vyborg captured. Hitler sent General Keitel and Ribbentrop to dissuade the Finns from seeking peace, but the Finnish president who had been associated with the German alliance was replaced by the old Finnish hero Marshal Mannerheim.

Negotiations were begun and in September a peace was signed. Finland had to pay reparations, had to accept a 50-year lease of

Pages 120-121: German troops pick their way along a Warsaw street.

Left: German troops after capturing a Warsaw barricade.

Below: A German officer gives orders during the Warsaw rising. The photograph was taken by a Pole.

territory west of Helsinki for a Russian base, and lost some other territory. The Finns were also required to help the Russians expel German forces from Finland, and some hard fighting was needed to accomplish this. But in general it was not a savage peace, probably because the previous Russo-Finnish War of 1939-40 had shown that Finns could be dangerous if pushed too far.

The German Army Group South Ukraine was increasingly vulnerable as army groups to the north of it were pushed westward. A further Soviet push into southern Poland or Hungary could cut it off, and army groups in Greece and Yugoslavia would also be imperiled. Hitler refused permission to withdraw, which gave the Red Army the opportunity it was seeking. In August two Russian army groups entered Rumania, trapping a German and a Rumanian army, and reaching the Danube after a week. The Rumanian King Michael dismissed the Antonescu government which, despite quarrels with Hitler, was still Germany's ally. Negotiations for peace did not move easily, but on August 23 Rumania surrendered and two days later declared war on Germany. After destroying the marooned German Sixth Army, the Russians entered Bucharest. By the end of September all of Rumania, with its oil and wheat, was in Russian hands, but by then most of the Russian strength had passed through the country and was engaged with the Germans in Hungary.

Two of the Russian armies moved southwest from Rumania to enter Bulgaria, which surrendered early in September and allied itself with Russia. This imperiled the German army group in Greece which, already fighting Greek partisans, was attacked by a Bulgarian army. It extricated itself in time and joined the army group holding Yugoslavia. These two army groups then formed support for the right flank of the Army Group South Ukraine which, no longer in the Ukraine, was attempting to keep the Russians out of Hungary. The Hungarian regent, Admiral Horthy, had decided to end his alliance with Hitler but had then been deposed by the Germans, who took direct control of the country. German resistance, however, was puny in comparison with the overwhelming Russian strength and zest. With the exception of the capital Budapest, where the Germans held out until late December, Hungary was taken, opening the way to Vienna. In Yugoslavia, Tito's partisans had taken control of Belgrade, which the Russians then entered in mid-October.

While the Soviet offensive was proceeding in southeastern Europe, another drive was taking place in the north, where the German Army Group North, forbidden to retreat earlier, was pushed into the Kurland peninsula. However, it was not completely cut off, because it could be supplied by sea.

Naval activity in the Russo-German war had been an auxiliary rather than a main interest of the contestants. Both regarded navies as essentially army-support forces, landing troops, frustrating enemy landings, and bringing gunfire to bear on coastal targets. During the war both sides also made great use of navies for evacuating their forces. In 1941, for example, the Red Navy lost three destroyers while rescuing a garrison from Hango in Finland, and the Black Sea Fleet supplied and then evacuated Odessa.

In both the Black Sea and the Baltic, the Red Navy was stronger than its opponents. In the former, the Germans were able to introduce submarines and light craft, but in the main they had to rely on air power to deter the Russian battleship, cruisers, and destroyers. In the Baltic the Russians began the war with two battleships, two modern cruisers, destroyers and submarines, and although in theory the Germans could have introduced superior forces, they had to retain some ships for the war against Britain. Moreover, they knew of the Russian efficiency in

minelaying and feared, too, that in the narrow waters of the eastern Baltic their heavy ships would suffer both from air attack and submarines.

In the Arctic waters the Soviet Northern Fleet mainly consisted of destroyers and submarines, and was employed in supporting the army in its struggle to keep the Germans from advancing on Murmansk, and in providing short-distance escorts for the convoys arriving from the West. For defense against any German battleships sent into Arctic waters the Russian relied mainly on the British navy, although in 1944 the British battleship *Royal Sovereign* was transferred to Russia and was stationed in the Arctic.

Unlike the Russian air force, the Red Navy had its own independent existence. But although on the eve of the war Stalin had been planning a big high seas fleet, the navy was still regarded simply as an adjunct of the army. When in 1941 German tanks approached Leningrad, they were assailed by 12-inch shells from a battleship. Even after a battleship had been sunk by dive-bombers in Leningrad harbor its long-range guns, remaining above water, continued to bombard German positions until the siege was lifted in 1944.

That was virtually the only activity of the Russian heavy ships in the Baltic. In 1944 the Germans did bring in some heavy ships, at first to bombard Russian troops advancing down the Baltic coast and then to protect the supply line to the German army group in Kurland. The Soviet heavy ships made no attempt to tackle them.

The Soviet offensive in the Baltic area was aided by several amphibious operations to land forces in the German rear. These were small-scale operations using light craft; motor torpedo boats, which had been disappointing in their intended role, were sometimes used, with infantrymen clinging to their bucking decks and no doubt glad when the time came to wade ashore.

As the Luftwaffe lost strength, the Red Navy's air arm became more effective in its attacks on German coastal shipping, making use of Boston torpedo-bombers supplied by the US. The Soviet attack technique resembled that of the Russian submarines and torpedo craft, with a marked reluctance to get close to the target and relying for a hit on a wide spread of missiles.

The Russian submarines in the Baltic were relatively inactive. Some submarines were lost in minefields and those that found targets launched torpedoes at too great a range for accuracy. Because the submarines were so

Above: Preparing to defend Budapest. German technicians service a King Tiger. The picture dramatically illustrates the development of tanks during World War II.

Right: Somewhere in Russia, willing hands pull a wounded German to the first-aid point on an improvised ambulance.

numerous the Germans and Finns laid a steel net across the neck of the Gulf of Finland, in an attempt to prevent them entering the broad expanses of the Baltic. In 1942 a few submarines had penetrated as far as Swedish coastal waters to prey on the iron-ore traffic destined for Germany. A few ships, including several flying the Swedish flag, were sunk in these expeditions.

In 1944 it was the German navy which had to play the role of savior, as pockets of cut-off troops requested evacuation by sea. These rescue operations were carried out by small craft, but to provide distant cover, and to bombard Russian army positions, a cruiser and two "pocket battleships" were brought in. The presence of the pocket battleships was no doubt a deterrent to any interference by Russian surface ships, but the absence of submarine attacks was surprising. There were some attacks by Russian naval aircraft, but these had little effect. Meanwhile the 600,000 men trapped in Kurland had to be supplied, and for several months this was accomplished with hardly any loss. Moreover, in 1945 the small remnant of the German navy would successfully oversee the evacuation of two million soldiers and refugees from various parts of the Baltic coast.

For some reason the Soviet Black Sea Fleet showed more initiative than the Baltic Fleet. The one battleship was used for coastal bombardments until its gun barrels wore out, and then was sent into retirement in a Caucasian port. The long siege of Odessa, which held up Hitler's plan for 1941, would have been impossible without the Soviet ships bringing supplies and reinforcements.

The navy also executed a successful landing behind the Rumanian troops' lines. Later, the Russian troops were successfully evacuated, with the navy taking most of them to defend Sevastopol which, again, was supplied by sea until its fall. In 1944 it was the turn of the Germans to evacuate the Crimea, and many eventually got away safely to a Rumanian port, despite the Russian submarines that had been placed to attack the evacuation ships. It was the last ships, harried by aircraft until their ammunition ran out, that suffered, and about 8000 German soldiers were drowned.

In 1944 there was a change in the pattern of naval activity in the far north. The Soviet port of Murmansk was only about 30 miles from the Norwegian and Finnish frontiers, both under German control. Yet the Germans had never succeeded in reaching that port. This was largely due to the series of successful landings made along the coast by the Soviets, and the supplying of a strong Russian force on the Rybachii peninsula, which prevented the German advance. Soviet light craft and submarines had continually preyed on the German seaborne supply routes. In 1944, with the defeat of Finland, the picture changed, with the Germans evacuating by sea and their supply convoys coming to an end.

By the end of 1944 Red Army personnel, including the air force, amounted to about seven million, and there were additional divisions supplied by Poles, Rumanians, Czechs and Bulgarians. The German Army, including SS formations, amounted to about two million on the Eastern Front. In the last half of the year it had lost about 800,000 men on the Eastern Front, as well as about 400,000 in Normandy. This was a loss that was not replaceable in the short term. Despite a lowering of quality, the German soldier and his officers were still superior in fighting abilities to the Russians and this, together with well-

chosen and well-organized defensive positions, did something to compensate for the numerical disparity.

However, Hitler's response to repeated reverses was to blame the army which, he increasingly implied, did not give him the support he deserved. He had always been fond of dismissing generals, if only to show he was the boss, but in 1944 his resentments took new directions. The firing squad for officers who authorized retreats in advance of permission from above became a common phenomenon in 1944. The same year it was announced that the families of such officers would also be punished. Nazi Party officials were appointed to army units in order to sniff out unenthusiastic officers and men. Some officers were compulsorily enrolled in the SS to enable more SS divisions to be formed, and Himmler gained more control over these units by the establishment of a separate SS Army HQ.

At the same time, Hitler became more willing to exploit the anti-Soviet army formed

Below: General von Manteuffel confers with colleagues in Rumania in spring 1944. Little-known before the war, Manteuffel was very impressive in his handling of several critical phases of the Russian campaign, and later would be selected by Hitler to command the armor in the Ardennes offensive. Cooperating with the Rumanians brought him little satisfaction.

from Russian prisoners of war. General Andrei Vlasov, one of the more popular and perceptive of the Soviet generals, had been captured in 1942 and encouraged by certain German officers to recruit anti-Soviet Russian soldiers among those who had been taken prisoner. Until 1944 Hitler had been reluctant to make great use of this potential source of troops – partly because it would not have looked good if despised Slavs fought alongside, perhaps even equaled, racially superior German units.

By 1944 the situation was desperate and Vlasov was authorized to form three divisions, but thanks to continuing German hesitation little use was made of them. In January 1945 a battalion of Vlasov's army would be sent against the Red Army in Silesia, with the result that even at that late stage of the war many Red soldiers deserted in order to change sides. At the end of the war Vlasov's men would be captured by the Americans, who returned them to Russia. Vlasov would be among them, destined to be

hung from a meat-hook in Moscow's Red Square.

The final big Russian offensive that was expected to bring the war to an end by the capture of Berlin was to be launched in December 1944, but Stalin postponed it because he thought colder weather would be worth waiting for. The mud and mists of December were not the best conditions for exploiting his superiority in tanks. It was finally launched on January 12. Zhukov had been appointed to lead this offensive as early as October, just after he had persuaded Stalin to postpone the capture of Warsaw. With his chief of staff, General M. S. Malinin, Zhukov planned the outline of this offensive during November only to find that, because of the postponement, he had time on his hands. With a five-to-one superiority in personnel and in tanks, a 17-to-one superiority in aircraft, and a seven-to-one superiority in guns and mortars, the success of the offensive was virtually guaranteed. Warsaw would be liberated in January and Berlin captured on May 2.

Below: Fresh German troops are airlifted during a critical phase of the Russian campaign in 1944. The aircraft is a tri-motor Junkers Ju 52, recognizable by its fluted metal fuselage. Introduced in the mid 1930s as a civil aircraft, it was soon adopted by the German forces and became their equivalent of the US Dakota.

HITLER'S LAST THROW

Previous pages: US
Sherman tanks pass
through a damaged village
during the advance
toward the German
frontier.

The surprise German offensive in the Ardennes, leading to the "Battle of the Bulge," was the critical event of the late 1944 campaign in Europe. But alarming and costly though it was, it was only an interlude, and it only temporarily interrupted the Allies' advance on Germany.

Patton's Third Army, after passing Paris, had taken Verdun and advanced to the Moselle where, in mid-September, it readied itself for an assault on Metz. Its southern flank now made contact with the US Seventh Army, which had advanced northward from the Mediterranean, while beyond the Seventh was the French First Army, waiting to advance on the eastern fortress towns of Belfort and Mulhouse. Up in the north, the British and Canadians, having reached Antwerp, were preparing to break into Germany through Holland, and between the British and Patton's army the central sector was covered by Bradley's US First and Ninth Armies.

Patton, like Montgomery, thought that a single, immediate, thrust could finish the war that year, but he also thought that the thrust should not be in the north, but on his own sector of the front. He therefore resented the order to adopt a defensive stance which he received in late September, just after he had captured Nancy. Knowledge that his slow-down was intended to make more resources available for Montgomery did not help matters, but Patton consoled himself by adopting a very broad interpretation of "defensive." He made no big offensives, but nevertheless contrived to launch several minor attack that could be described as consolidations.

Meanwhile Eisenhower was deciding where the main weight of the offensive should be placed. Montgomery, naturally enough and with some strategic justification, argued that the north was still the crucial sector. Bradley thought his own army group, of which Patton's force was a part, should have

a major role. Eisenhower decided that there should be a two-pronged assault, one through Holland and the other against two industrial areas, the Ruhr and the Saar.

Patton's staff had already done much of the planning for this advance, so the Third Army was ready some weeks before Montgomery, and began its advance without waiting for the British on November 8. Metz was captured 10 days later, but rain and then snow slowed down the Americans. By December 15 the Third Army was almost in sight of the main town, Saarbrucken. It had reached the Siegfried Line in many places and at one point had driven 30 miles beyond it. The capital of Alsace, Strasbourg, had been taken. In this sector the Seventh Army, marching from the south, also participated while the French First Army moved east to take Belfort and Mulhouse. The Seventh Army and the French lost touch in their respective advances, so an unconquered pocket was left around Colmar.

Above: Dutch girls chalk welcoming words on one of the Polish tanks that liberated Breda.

Far left: On the lookout for trouble, a US infantryman, supported by a tank, covers a street in the course of liberating a French town.

Left: In Belfort, close to the frontier with Germany in eastern France, a French soldier aims his light machine gun at a suspected German position.

Left: Men of the Seaforth Highlanders, with Canadian driver, during the advance toward Hertogenbosh in Holland. These "Kangaroo" transport vehicles were reconstructed tanks.

Below: Vickers heavy machine guns, used by the British in two world wars, in a Dutch landscape near Hertogenbosh.

Left: US troops carefully investigate a Belgian town close to the German frontier, September 1944.

On the whole, German resistance was stronger than expected; the few weeks of respite had allowed the Germans to regroup, regain their morale, and replace losses. Since the Americans had far more resources, with fresh divisions arriving almost every week, this was not felt to be a great threat, because in a battle of attrition the weaker side inevitably comes off worse. For the British, however, who had reached their limit, battles of attrition could not be accepted, and this to some extent explains why the British government, for the most part, favored Montgomery's proposals for a quick finish to the war. This was not true of British staff officers, many of whom were as exasperated by Mont-

gomery as were the Americans. British staff officers working in Eisenhower's Supreme Headquarters were among these, but more powerful British influences were Air Chief Marshal Tedder, Eisenhower's deputy for the Allied air forces, and Admiral Bertram Ramsay, who had already done wonders in organizing the naval side of the Normandy landings. At a meeting of army group commanders, and the naval and air commanders which Eisenhower called in early October, Ramsay was incensed when Montgomery declared that the Allies could capture the Ruhr without first gaining the use of Antwerp. Ramsay exploded, and blamed Montgomery for the faulty strategy of according priority to a knock-out blow against Germany rather than to securing a decent port for supplies. Brooke, the Chief of the Imperial General Staff, who usually supported Montgomery, did not, and his silence was probably more influential than Ramsay's attack.

Eisenhower, then and later, took the blame for the faulty strategy that had caused a supply crisis, on the grounds that he had approved Montgomery's Arnhem operation at a time when all resources should have been devoted to Antwerp. The situation at the time of this meeting was that the Allied armies were close to the German frontiers, but their supplies were still largely landed on French beaches; Cherbourg was becoming operable, but had a limited throughput, while Boulogne and Calais, captured in late September, were only small.

Above: A varied collection of landing craft after the Walcheren landing at Westkapelle. Also visible are three of the standard German beach obstacles. One of the armored bulldozers, most of which got stuck in the clay, is in the foreground.

In the days following this meeting, Eisenhower bombarded Montgomery with messages emphasizing that without Antwerp the Allied advance would have to come to a halt in November. In return, Montgomery bombarded the Supreme Commander with messages advocating his ideas for changing the chain of command. But eventually, after Eisenhower had called on the moral support of both the US and British chiefs of staff, Montgomery pigeonholed his organizational proposals and started planning a campaign to open Antwerp.

Antwerp was a large well-equipped port, but ships reached it through the long Scheldt estuary, which was commanded along its northern shore by the islands of South Beveland and Walcheren, and on its southern shore by another part of occupied Holland. Montgomery's first move was to push the Germans out of the southern shore, thereby opening a path for a seaborne assault of Walcheren if that should prove necessary. An alternative line of attack was from the east, through South Beveland and over the causeway into Walcheren.

Above: A Sherman tank advances through the damaged Dutch town of Overloon. The Shermans were the mainstay of the Allied armored forces, serving not only the US army but also the Poles. The British, whose tank design and construction rates were not as good, also acquired many Shermans.

to be the most important battle of the campaign, which in some ways it was, their top commanders acted as though this was not so. For Rundstedt, seeing Allied armies poised against his homeland in a line from the North Sea down to the Swiss frontier, and with his front line stretched by the Nijmegen salient carved out by the paratroopers, there was perhaps strong emotional cause for ignoring the fact that the surest way of holding the Allies was to deny them their supply routes; as by this stage both Rundstedt and other generals felt that it was time to make peace, there might also have been some logic in their approach.

Be that as it may, it is remarkable that the defense of Walcheren was entrusted to the "White Bread Division," a formation thus termed because it consisted of men who, succumbing to real or imagined digestive disorders on the Eastern Front, had been sent to the Netherlands to enjoy the benefit of the local diet. The German naval officers felt they had a far better appreciation of the situation than the military, and resented a situation in which their carefully sited guns had the protection only of convalescent and not very military soldiers.

Both Beveland and Walcheren were below sea level, and were intersected by dykes and drainage canals. Roads ran over the dykes but were usually very narrow. Walcheren was preserved from the sea by tall dunes that lined its coast, supplemented by strong dykes at some places. Commanders of both sides realized that it would be easy to flood these areas simply by breaching the dykes, but it was not always certain whether the

The aim was to capture or eliminate the German coastal guns on Walcheren. These guns, operated by the German navy, covered the Scheldt and thereby prevented any attempt to clear the minefield that blocked the estuary. Until those mines were cleared, Antwerp was useless.

By this time Rundstedt had been restored to command of the German western armies. Somehow, like Montgomery, he did not give Antwerp top priority. Although at this period both the British and German troops in this sector were being told that this was going

Right: The channel separating Walcheren from Beveland, where the British and Canadians found a crossing place. As the battle goes on, the wounded and German prisoners are brought back.

Below: Another badly damaged French town, Bining, is entered by the Americans, December 1944.

attack or the defense would most benefit by this. In the event, the German defenders flooded much of South Beveland, while the British put all of Walcheren under water.

For defenders, flooding forced attackers to stay on the high land, which was usually the dykes, where they could easily be taken under fire. For attackers, flooding hampered the quick movement of reinforcements, and most defenses depended on this swift movement of troops to plug breakthroughs. One thing was certain, tanks were of no use to either defenders or attackers.

In South Beveland Canadian infantry, confined by flooding to virtually one route, pressed forward slowly but, while mastering the island, were unable to continue onward into Walcheren. The causeway linking the two islands was about 40 feet wide, 1200 yards long, and dead straight. A number of attempts were made to force this obstacle, but eventually the idea was given up. Later, after landings had been made in Walcheren, a way was found across the water using shallows instead of the causeway.

For a seaborne assault on Walcheren, which was increasingly seen to be necessary if the Scheldt was to be cleared in November, two alternative landing places were chosen. One was the small port of Flushing, directly facing the Scheldt, and the other was the beaches at Westkapelle. The planners found that it was the German navy rather than the German army which posed the worst problems. The anti-shipping minefields in the Scheldt were not the only mines laid by the

Germans. The coasts were also protected, usually with different types of ground mines that exploded when a ship passed nearby, but could have a delayed actuation which allowed one or two ships, minesweepers preferably, to pass before the mines became active.

As for the guns, these mainly followed the navy's preference for siting right on the coast, with direct firing. There were a few situated inland, for indirect fire, and when the dykes were broken these would be flooded. Most of the anti-aircraft guns protecting the gun sites were also set back, but the bigger and more dangerous guns (5.9-inch) were on the dunes, encased in thick layers of concrete. Experience off Normandy, not to speak of Gallipoli in 1915, suggested that only direct hits by battleship guns would wreck these, although near misses or hits by lighter guns could put them out of action for short periods.

British Lancaster and Mosquito aircraft dropped 1270 tons of bombs on the Westkapelle sea dyke on October 3. Although much of the village was flattened, enough bombs had found their target to ensure that by nightfall there was a 75-yard gap in the dyke, through which the sea was flowing. Emergency dams built to contain the floods proved useless, for Bomber Command returned for more dyke-breaking on October 7. Leaflets had been dropped on October 2, warning the local population to leave, but the Germans had turned back the flow of refugees seeking safety outside the island. However, most went to the local capital, Middelburg, where the ground was slightly higher. Probably about 200 islanders were drowned, less than feared.

The Dutch Resistance had been warned that its services might soon be required, but with the flooded terrain air drops of weapons were impracticable. Some Dutchmen assured worried German officers that the water would rise to the rooftops; having thereby persuaded them to seek temporary safety elsewhere, the Dutch could purloin their weapon and munition stocks with very little difficulty.

Above: At the start of the Ardennes offensive, German troops hurry across a road blocked by guns and burning vehicles. At this stage of the battle, the Germans still had their old confidence.

Left: A ditched US half-track, occupied by two German soldiers, is passed by a German personnel carrier advancing into a Belgian village.

Right: One of the best-known pictures of this period: the main street of Bastogne, crowded with the vehicles so essential for the US operations. This street still stands today very much unchanged, but handling a different kind of traffic.

Below: US troops manhandling their antitank gun in the mud close to the Belgian-German frontier.

In the end, the British decided to land both at Flushing and Westkapelle. The Flushing assault was to be covered by artillery on the opposite shore of the Scheldt. Having learned nothing, apparently, from the experience at Caen, where turning the town into rubble held up rather than speeded the Allied advance, the planning staff requested heavy bomber attacks to soften up the defenses. The British Chiefs of Staff, and Churchill, wisely turned down this request, but on humanitarian grounds; Flushing, after all, was not an enemy town.

The Flushing landing was successful, and the street by street fighting which ensued was patchy. Sometimes exuberant Dutch civilians, bewildered and armed Germans, and tense British commandos were inextricably mixed up. Germans were usually eager to surrender, but here and there isolated pockets of diehards put up stiff resistance. Having gained Flushing, the British (largely Scots and Canadians) awaited the expected orders to move along the elevated main road to Middelburg, where the local German commander had his headquarters.

Meanwhile, at Westkapelle successful landings were much more dependent on air support, designed to quell the several batteries that could fire directly on the approaching landing craft and on the beaches themselves. Heavy bombers as well as tactical fighter-bombers were used, but such operations were limited to days when the weather was suitable both on the airfields, in Britain mainly, and over Walcheren. Only one or two guns were put out of action by bombing, but command posts and radar installations also suffered. Naval bombardments using the 15-inch guns of the battleship *Warspite* and two monitors were also requested, although not perfectly executed.

The naval authorities in the Thames were told to prepare at a very late date, so the monitors did not have time to make a second trip after exhausting their ammunition; one of them, moreover, was soon out of action with a mechanical fault. *Warspite*'s gun barrels were worn and therefore lacking in accuracy. Furthermore, the very small statistical chance of a shell making a direct hit should have recommended concentration of fire on just one or two of the most dangerous enemy guns, but fire was divided and it was only by good fortune that a monitor did hit one of the heavy batteries. *Warspite* fired hundreds of shells, but did not score a direct hit.

After the final naval and air strikes the landing craft went in, aimed at two beaches at each side of the gap that had been made in the sea dyke at Westkapelle. The operation was enlivened by some rocket-firing support craft, which contrived to drop their patterns of rockets among the advancing landing craft. This caused little damage, but some confusion and anger. A number of landing craft were sunk by the enemy in this vulnerable stage, despite the efforts of RAF Typhoons to confuse and quell the German guns.

British commandos, including Belgian and Norwegian sections, soon fought their way into Westkapelle village and, although there had been serious casualties in the initial stages of the assault, progress was henceforth quite brisk, the Germans being unable to move reinforcements swiftly. German soldiers were no longer so keen to respond to "fight to the last man" exhortations – they had heard it all too many times before. By the end of the day six miles of beach were in the possession of the commandos. The amphibious Buffalo vehicles, big tracked personnel carriers invented by the Americans for assaults over coral reefs, had shown their worth in crossing the beaches, although they could not cope with steep dunes and were very vulnerable to landmines. Other vehicles had been less useful, and much specialized equipment had been lost while being landed. Five of the six armored bulldozers that the sappers intended to use for mine clearance were put out of action, mainly by getting stuck in underwater clay. Supply vessels continued to suffer loss from German shellfire. However, on November 2 the beachhead was further extended.

Dutch Resistance forces conveyed to the British in Flushing that the German commander, ensconced in Middelburg, was prepared to surrender but really needed the approach of British armored forces to provide

Above: The German Ardennes offensive failed above all because of a lack of fuel supplies. This is a German King Tiger tank. It ran out of fuel in mid-campaign and its crew hoisted a white flag.

Left: The extremes of the Ardennes landscape are clearly portrayed in this picture of US infantrymen of the 4th Armored Division advancing toward Bastogne.

they best knew, while the Germans, to keep up their spirits, began to sing patriotic songs, including the notorious Nazi *Horst Wessel* song. It was an inflammatory mixture: indignant German officers, maudlin German soldiers, half-drunk vengeful Dutch, and a small group of British soldiers, all on the same square. This, perhaps, was the finest hour of the Dutch Resistance, which organized its men, removed the drunks, disarmed the potentially violent, and got the local bakers to make bread for the hungry Germans.

By November 8 the commando tactic of advancing during the night had worn down the remaining German units on the island, and the senior German commander surrendered. After that, the difficult task of minesweeping began, and on the 26th the first supply ships docked in Antwerp. Securing the Scheldt had delayed Montgomery's thrust toward the Ruhr, but the US Third and Seventh Armies had started their advance, the other prong of the Allied offensive, just as Walcheren was captured.

Hitler was already planning what was later seen to be his last throw, a surprise counteroffensive through the hilly, wooded Ardennes toward Antwerp. The surprise would consist of two elements: the choice of the Ardennes, where the terrain was regarded as highly unsuitable for tanks, and the fact that it took place at all. Although German resistance was growing, the Allied commanders did not feel that Hitler could gather enough strength for a major operation; most of the German commanders felt the same, but did not have the strength of will needed to cope with Hitler's obstinate optimism.

By this time German males between the ages of 15 and 60 were being recruited into the army, and despite the critical situation on the Eastern Front, Hitler held back for his Ardennes offensive some valuable formations, including experienced panzer divisions. In one way or another, he found 28 divisions, totaling 250,000 men, and nine of them were armored. The 2500 available tanks were not really sufficient, but they included the Mark V Panthers and Mark VI Tigers, which were superior to the US Shermans in guns and armor. In any case, it would have been difficult to maintain fuel supply for a greater number of tanks. The main German weakness was in the air; dominance by the US Air Force meant that supplies for the advancing Germans, which were short in any case, would be very vulnerable. However, bad flying weather could be expected in December.

an excuse. Not having any tanks, the British sent a group of amphibious Buffaloes into Middelburg. These were more vulnerable than tanks, and one of them was shattered by a mine, but the others got through. They entered Middelburg noisily, with Typhoons circling overhead, and there was no opposition. They then drew up in the main square, where German troops were assembling. Nobody seemed to want to start a battle, so the British major went to find the German commander and persuaded him to surrender, threatening the destruction of Middelburg in case of refusal. The German, who at that stage did not realize the weakness of the British force, agreed.

An hour later, German staff officers discovered how weak the British were, while more Germans assembled on the square, some formed up in units. All around the square the Dutch were celebrating in the way

The Ardennes had been the scene of one of Hitler's Blitzkrieg triumphs in 1940, and it is perhaps surprising that the Allies placed so much confidence in the forbidding terrain, which they covered with only four divisions. In fact, it was possible for tanks to cross this area, provided they stayed on the high ground, while the woods provided excellent cover for other arms.

The few German commanders who knew what Hitler was planning tried to head him off with a more limited offensive, but he did not want to listen. Not only was he confident of repeating the 1940 success, but sure that such a success would lead not only to a delay in the Allied advance, if only because Antwerp would be regained, but also to the split between the Allies on which he had long counted. In preceding weeks the US and British press had been full of partisan comment on the differences between Montgomery and Eisenhower, and on how one side or the other was not pulling its weight, and Hitler regarded this as further evidence that if only the Allies were put under more strain they would cease to be allies.

The differences between the Allied generals were, of course, minor compared to the split among the Germans. The July Plot against Hitler had divided the top commanders into those who had been presented with complimentary doses of poison, and those who had survived. Rommel, probably the best of all, had swallowed his prescription. Guderian, also outstanding in his generalship, had chosen the low road, lashed out at "traitorous" generals who knew of the plot but kept quiet, and had survived. But his field was the Eastern Front, and he was not happy at the prospect of valuable reserves being dissipated against the Americans. Even generals loyal to Hitler had been horrified at the barbarously cruel deaths meted out to the hundreds of officers arrested for direct complicity in the plot.

The spirit of suspicion, fear and resentment was well expressed in the arrangements Hitler made to meet the commanders of the formations earmarked for his Ardennes offensive. Until this meeting, everything had been kept secret from them and then, a few days before the operation was scheduled to start, they were assembled, put into a motorcoach which rumbled around the countryside near Frankfurt until they had lost all sense of direction, and then deposited them outside Hitler's local bunker. Only when they were disarmed, and deprived of their attache cases, were they allowed into the Führer's presence. Just four days later,

December 16, they began their advance. One panzer army was to attack northwest, skirting the Ardennes, to Antwerp, while the other, to the south, was to push through the Ardennes region and then turn north toward Antwerp.

The Germans' northern advance under Dietrich's SS Panzer Army, thanks to its battleworthiness and the unexpectedness of its onslaught against the US V Corps, pushed back the Americans at several points, but could not make a long-distance break-

Above: B-26 Marauder bombers are prepared for action. Although low cloud over the Ardennes cleared for a few vital days, low temperatures required extra efforts to maintain serviceability.

through. Some of its advance units got to within a mile of a huge US fuel dump which, if captured, would have made an enormous contribution to the German effort, for several times in the ensuing days German armored formations were compelled to halt because of fuel shortages.

In the Ardennes proper, Manteuffel's Fifth Panzer Army was more successful. The US divisions which faced him were not only few, but consisted mainly of resting or freshly arrived units. Both unprepared and un-equipped for proper battle, many US troops surrendered, but others fought to the end. There were enough of these small-scale heroic last stands to slow down the Germans, which, as things turned out, was crucial.

The key German need was to cover enough ground before the Americans could collect themselves and interpose strong units to block the panzers. Realizing this, a well-organized disinformation operation had been set up in which American-speaking Germans in US uniforms penetrated behind the US lines. Some started rumors (the one about a plot to assassinate Eisenhower using men dressed as US soldiers caused enormous security problems, practically cutting off Eisenhower from the outside world), while others posed as traffic cops at road junctions, blithely despatching US reinforcements in the wrong direction. It was some time before these agents could be arrested and executed.

Right: Bastogne is relieved after the epic and decisive siege which did much to blunt the German offensive in the Ardennes.

Above: German soldiers in American custody in late 1944.

Above right: This map of the Battle of the Bulge suggests that Hitler was not wildly wrong when he launched his offensive. Having the good fortune of bad weather, the German advance was deep and it was probably only lack of fuel that prevented German armor reaching the Meuse. How a victory might have benefited Hitler in the long term, however, is hard to visualize. It might have won him a few extra weeks but that would merely have prolonged the German agony.

Right: A US artillery battery prepares for a fire mission.

Far right: The thick woods of the Ardennes and low winter temperatures seriously hampered tank operations.

In the meantime Americans in the battle zone who strayed from their companies were not only coping with enemy bullets but with demands from their own side for proof that they were genuine Americans.

For the first few days fortune favored the Germans, because the weather was poor. Within 48 hours Manteuffel's panzers reached the key road junction of Bastogne. Here, however, the US 10th Armored Division had arrived just in time, and held on grimly. Manteuffel was able to pass his divisions around Bastogne, but the delay enabled the Americans to bring up reserves.

At the time of the German attack Patton's staff had been preparing their own offensive, but immediately began to plan new moves to deal with Manteuffel. So when Eisenhower summoned the Third Army into action it was ready. Eisenhower had decided that the US First and Ninth Armies, cut off in the north by the German advance, should be placed under Montgomery's command. While Montgomery would press down on the Germans from the north, threatening their supply routes, the US Third Army would move up from the south, making above all for Bastogne, which had become so important for the German communications.

It took Patton much longer than he had expected to relieve Bastogne, but the tenacity of the Americans besieged there had slowed down the German drive. On December 23 the skies cleared, and Allied air power was brought into the equation for a few precious days. The German generals realized that their offensive would not now succeed, but Hitler was not convinced of this. On December 26 Patton finally relieved Bastogne. But then the weather closed in again, giving the Germans the chance to renew attacks against this vital center.

Meanwhile, in the north, Montgomery was at his best, stabilizing a difficult situation. Told by Eisenhower to hold the line of the Meuse, withdrawing here and there to shorten the line, and then prepare his forces for a counterattack, Montgomery performed brilliantly. However, General Bradley, among others, resented the temporary transfer of two of his armies to Montgomery's command. To General Hodges, in charge of the US First Army that had now fallen to Montgomery's command, he sent the advice to ignore Montgomery's orders if he did not agree with them. What Montgomery did was to bring down his own British units to secure the line of the Meuse, while Hodges delayed the German advance and prepared his units for a counterstroke. The German armored divisions, repeatedly held up waiting for fuel, in fact never reached the Meuse, although one division, far ahead of the others, almost reached Dinant.

Montgomery chose just the right moment to launch his counter-offensive, so by the end of December the Germans found themselves with a salient that was under strong attack from both north and south. There was really no alternative to a withdrawal, although it would be February before the Ardennes were cleared. The Battle of the Bulge, as the Americans called it, had cost the Germans over 100,000 men, but American losses had been heavy too, at about 80,000 killed, wounded, and captured.

In retrospect, the reasons for the German failure lay in the unexpected tenacity of some US units in the early days, including units that had never been in action before. Then there was the superb staffwork of Patton's Third Army, which enabled him to send relieving forces much earlier than the Germans had expected. Finally there was Montgomery's success in patching up a dire situation in the north. As was to be expected, it was not long before Montgomery was claiming that he had saved the US bacon. But while acrimony continued, and would continue after the war, the fact remained that the Allied generals, despite their clashes, had succeeded in quelling Hitler's final attempt at Blitzkrieg. On this front, as the German generals well knew, the war was lost. As for the Eastern Front, in many ways more frightening, the effort put into the Ardennes operation meant that there was less strength with which to face the Russians.

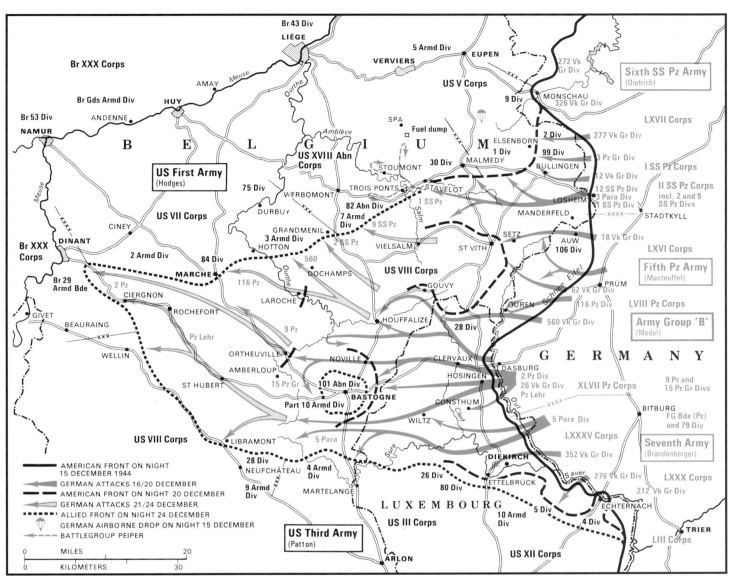

US First Army (Hodges)

Br XXX Corps

Br 43 Div
LIÈGE
VERVIERS
5 Armd Div
EUPEN
US V Corps
272 Vk Gr Div
Sixth SS Pz Army (Dietrich)

AMAY
Meuse
9 Div
MONSCHAU
326 Vk Gr Div
LXVII Corps

Br Gds Armd Div
HUY
ANDENNE
Ourthe
SPA
Fuel dump
Ambléve
2 Div
277 Vk Gr Div

Br 53 Div
NAMUR
B E L G
STOUMONT
US XVIII Abn Corps
I U M
ELSENBORN
1 Div
MALMEDY
99 Div
BULLINGEN
3 Pz Gr Div
12 Vk Gr Div
I SS Pz Corps

Meuse
30 Div
TROIS PONTS
STAVELOT
Salm
12 SS Pz Div
3 Para Div
1 SS Pz Div
LOSHEIM
II SS Pz Corps incl. 2 and 9 SS Pz Divs

75 Div
WERBOMONT
1 SS Pz
MANDERFELD
STADTKYLL

DINANT
CINEY
US VII Corps
DURBUY
82 Abn Div
7 Armd Div
9 SS Pz
SETZ
18 Vk Gr Div

Br XXX Corps
2 Armd Div
84 Div
MARCHE
GRANDMENIL
3 Armd Div
HOTTON
2 SS Pz
VIELSALM
ST VITH
AUW
106 Div
LXVI Corps
Fifth Pz Army (Manteuffel)

Br 29 Armd Bde
2 Pz
CIERGNON
Ourthe
560
DOCHAMPS
US VIII Corps
GOUVY
Schnee Eifel
PRÜM
62 Vk Gr Div
LVIII Pz Corps

GIVET
ROCHEFORT
116 Pz
LAROCHE
HOUFFALIZE
DUREN
116 Pz Div
560 Vk Gr Div
Army Group 'B' (Model)

BEAURAING
Pz Lehr
9 Pz
28 Div
G E R M A N Y

WELLIN
ORTHEUVILLE
NOVILLE
CLERVAUX
DASBURG
2 Pz Div
26 Vk Gr Div
Pz Lehr
XLVII Pz Corps
9 Pz and 15 Pz Gr Divs

ST HUBERT
AMBERLOUP
15 Pz Gr
101 Abn Div
BASTOGNE
HOSINGEN
CONSTHUM
BITBURG
FG Bde (Pz) and 79 Div

Part 10 Armd Div
WILTZ
Clerf
Our
5 Para Div
LXXXV Corps
Seventh Army (Brandenberger)

LIBRAMONT
5 Para
DIEKIRCH
352 Vk Gr Div

US VIII Corps
NEUFCHÂTEAU
28 Div
4 Armd Div
Sure
26 Div
ETTELBRUCK
80 Div
276 Vk Gr Div
LXXX Corps

MARTELANGE
9 Armd Div
Sauer
5 Div
ECHTERNACH
212 Vk Gr Div

US Third Army (Patton)
L U X E M B O U R G
10 Armd Div
US III Corps
4 Div
TRIER
LIII Corps

ARLON
US XII Corps

AMERICAN FRONT ON NIGHT 15 DECEMBER 1944
GERMAN ATTACKS 16/20 December
AMERICAN FRONT ON NIGHT 20 December
GERMAN ATTACKS 21/24 December.
ALLIED FRONT ON NIGHT 24 December
GERMAN AIRBORNE DROP ON NIGHT 15 DECEMBER
BATTLEGROUP PEIPER

MILES 20
KILOMETERS 30

THE BOMBER OFFENSIVE

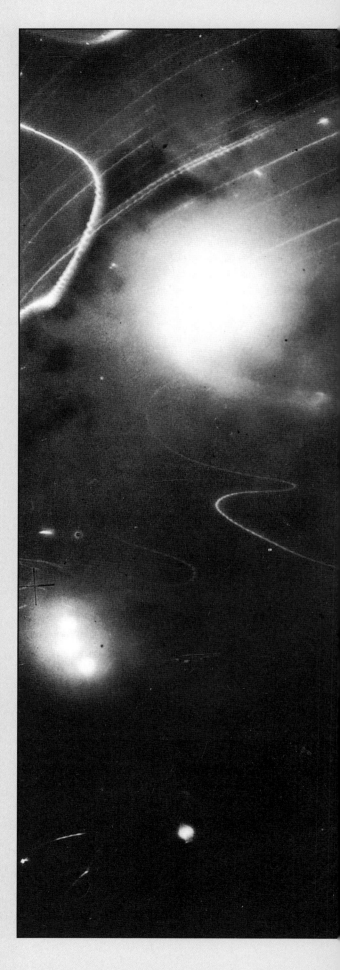

Right: A four-engined bomber, mainstay of the US and British strategic air forces. The Axis powers did not often go beyond two-engined machines.

Left: A US bomber crew at one of its briefings.

Far left: The crew of a B-24 Liberator bomber wearily leave their aircraft after returning to their British airbase after a raid on Germany. Not as well-armed as the B-17 and less agile, these aircraft were nevertheless produced in large numbers both for the USAAF and for the RAF. RAF Transport Command was engaged largely in ferrying these aircraft across the Atlantic.

In January 1943 Roosevelt and Churchill had met at the Casablanca Conference, and one of the decisions they had to make was how to handle their growing strategic bomber force. Already the US 8th Air Force had moved its bombers into airfields in eastern Britain to supplement the RAF's Bomber Command. By then both forces used four-engined bombers for, practically alone among the powers, Britain and the USA had long pursued a policy of building specialized strategic bombers.

Whereas Hitler in his bombing of Britain had relied on twin-engined machines that were mainly designed for ground-support operations, the B-17 Flying Fortresses and B-24 Liberators of the US Air Force, and the Lancasters of the RAF, could carry very heavy bomb loads over long distances and, at least in the American view, enough defensive guns to keep enemy fighters at a reasonable distance.

The weak point of Allied bombers was that they were usually unable to hit their target. The actual percentage of bombs that fell within damaging distance of a target varied according to conditions, and also to the techniques of the specialists and statisticians making the calculations. The worst finding

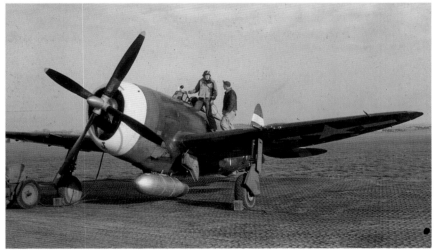

was that only three bombs in every 100 fell within 100 yards of the target, but even the more optimistic findings were almost as bad. The dive-bomber, so beloved by Hitler, had a much better hit-ratio but the British did not favor this technique, and in any case the dive-bomber with its limited range and its single bomb was of little use for strategic bombing. Quite apart from that, as German Stuka pilots had discovered after the triumphs of 1940-41, the dive-bomber was encountering much more effective countermeasures.

Above: The P-47 Thunderbolt was one of the best-known fighters of World War II. This example was photographed in England; its range was sufficient to escort 8th Air Force bombers as far as Belgium.

In both Britain and America the primacy of strategic bombing had been urged on politicians and the press well before the war, and there was therefore a ready audience for the claims of the bombing enthusiasts. Many of the latter believed that bombing alone could win the war, provided only that sufficient resources were allocated to it. Until the beginning of 1944 the heavy bomber services, although they never received all that they asked for, were by and large satisfied. Churchill, for one, believed in top priority for the bomber until a quite late stage of the war.

Yet by 1943 some doubts were filtering into political minds. As time would show, the bomber was indeed a very important weapon, and in the final campaign against Japan in 1945, when improved bombing techniques were used against highly-inflammable residential areas, it would probably have brought victory even without the atomic bombs. But 1943-44 showed that Germany would not be brought to surrender merely by conventional bombing.

With their Norden bombsights, American bombers were somewhat more accurate than

Below: A Lancaster four-engined bomber of the RAF. The underside blister houses the "H2S" radar scanner that produced a rough indication of the main physical features on the ground.

British in the early years of the war, but as the British equipped themselves with better technology their accuracy also increased. It was not merely a question of hitting a target but of navigating to the target city. There were RAF raids on the Ruhr (where cities were quite close to each other) when only one-tenth of the bombers actually arrived over their target city. Most of them bombed the wrong city, without knowing. Radio-beam aids to navigation were not favored, largely because the German navigation beams had been disrupted by the British in 1940-41.

Devices like "H2S," "Oboe" and "Window" did, however, after initial development problems, improve the accuracy of both RAF and American navigation. Unfortunately, the chief of Bomber Command, Arthur Harris, by that time was so wedded to the concept that his bombers could not hit precise targets that he was unable to appreciate the value of new devices and stayed with his old tactics of area bombing, whose rationale was that if only a tiny percentage of bombs hit their target those targets could still be hit if only enough bombs were dropped.

Below: Another four-engined RAF bomber, the Halifax. This aircraft is taking part in a daylight raid against a Ruhr synthetic oil plant in 1944.

Above: B-17 Flying Fortresses of the 8th Air Force over England, where they were based for much of the war. Although superseded by the B-29 Superfortresses, these aircraft were in frontline service throughout the war, but their powerful gun armament was never quite enough to deter German fighters.

The essential weakness of Harris's policy was that it was not usually followed to its logical conclusion. Instead of picking an important industrial or military target Harris preferred to direct his bombers to city centers. This was partly because, whatever he might say about military and industrial targets, his real object was to hit and demoralize civilians. It was also simpler. Aiming for city centers did at least ease the navigation problem at a time when the rapid inflow of new aircrew meant that most navigators were inexperienced.

The navigational problems would have been easier to solve in daylight but Harris, quite rightly, realized that his bombers would be much more at the mercy of enemy fighters and anti-aircraft guns in daylight. Darkness was Bomber Command's greatest asset. Losses were very heavy in any case. Although the survival rate of Bomber Command aircrew was somewhat better than that of German U-boat crews, it was not much better. Some airmen did survive throughout the several years of the bombing campaign, but they were lucky.

For publicity reasons, Berlin was frequently a target for British bombers, even though it was not very rewarding, with strong defenses and widely-spaced targets. Harris preferred older towns where the centers were congested and largely of

Above: A P-51 Mustang fighter, whose extra, jettisonable, fuel tanks enabled it to escort bombers over Germany.

great success in its ostensible task of wrecking German industry. Factories tended to be located not in city centers, but in suburbs, and therefore were not greatly damaged. There were important exceptions to this tale of ineffectiveness, however. A raid against Peenemünde on the Baltic coast was made in a vague belief that something vital might be achieved, and so many bombs were dropped that the program of developing the V-2 rocket was slowed considerably. In this instance Bomber Command did not realize until later that it had made an important contribution – it was the delayed development of the V-2 that enabled Britain in late 1944 to escape comparatively lightly from this new and potentially devastating weapon.

Partly because industrial targets were not badly hit, Hitler considered that Bomber Command in fact was not trying to hit industrial areas, and he therefore neglected protective measures. He was very reluctant to sanction night-fighter production and neither he nor Goering ever took seriously the establishment of a properly equipped and coordinated fighter defense system. The German response to Harris's attacks on small, easily combustible towns was Hitler's personal reaction, and initially took the form of attacks on Britain's easily combustible towns.

The so-called "Little Blitz," the new bombing offensive against Britain in response to Bomber Command's activities, was therefore terror-bombing aimed at ancient towns of little industrial, but considerable cultural, value. As Germany still did not have a heavy strategic bomber it was again twin-engined

wooden construction, and where the defences were weaker. Incendiary bombs were dropped, and then high explosives to kill the firefighters. In 1943 and 1944 the firestorm became a Bomber Command speciality, with areas made to burn so fiercely that the combustion produced high winds which raised the temperatures even higher; by this time Bomber Command was not simply burning, but was cremating, Germans by the thousands.

In the case of the massive raids against Hamburg, civilian casualties were numbered in the scores of thousands. Yet although Germans began to despair, their morale did not collapse. Nor could Bomber Command claim

aircraft that were used in these campaigns of 1942 and 1943-44. Nor were many aircraft available; the bigger raids using only about 150 aircraft. In 1940, 600 such medium bombers had been sent at one time against Britain. So these German counterattacks had little effect.

The American Air Force had polite reservations about Bomber Command's strategy. Possessing, it thought, aircraft that had little to fear from fighters, and a bombsight that guaranteed a high proportion of hits so long as the target was visible, it logically preferred daylight raids against specific targets.

The leaders and chiefs of staff assembled at Casablanca in early 1943 were only hazily aware of how successful, or unsuccessful, the strategic bombing campaign was proving. This was partly because intelligence information was scarce, and partly because wishful thinking impelled the bombing services to downgrade reports that did not conform with the expectation that all those thousands of tons of bombs must bring decisive results.

On the other hand, both Churchill and Roosevelt were aware of the arguments against the existing pattern of strategic bombing, for the army and navy chiefs made no secret of their belief that money spent on strategic bombing would be better spent on more support for their own services. As post-war research has shown, they were quite right. At some periods Britain was devoting 25 percent, and the USA 15 percent, of the war effort to the maintenance of the bombing offensive, and in both cases this was about four times more than the value of the damage caused by the two bomber forces.

In the end a compromise program was adopted at Casablanca, called "Pointblank." This seems to have been devised to please both the US and British bomber services, but also moved in the direction of giving greater emphasis to work that would directly assist the armies and navies. Specific classes of target were noted, the U-boat construction yards being at the top of the list.

Aircraft factories, transportation facilities, and oil refineries were also listed, and there was provision for attacks on lesser industries that were vital for the German armaments industry. Having enumerated these specific

targets, which were in line with US Air Force policy, Pointblank took care to soothe Bomber Command by attributing great importance to area bombing by night.

In effect, this provided a program for round-the-clock bombing of Germany, with the RAF's nocturnal sledgehammer falling between heavy daylight assaults by the American 8th Air Force, which from October was joined by the 9th Air Force operating bombing missions against Germany from airfields in Italy. But the Pointblank program soon met obstacles. While Bomber Command continued with its night attacks on civilian centers and persuaded itself that the quite high sacrifice of qualified aircrew was justified by the results obtained, the US precision bombing missions did not go according to expectations.

An early raid against Wilhelmshaven, where U-boats were assembled, did very little damage and was quite costly. Although much of the Luftwaffe's fighter force was on the Eastern Front, enough German fighters were available to show that US bombers were not, as had been hoped, fully capable of protecting themselves. Fighters fitted with cannons in place of machine guns were, by 1943, the rule rather than the exception, and they had a great advantage in range and destructive power over the machine guns mounted in US bombers. In summer 1943 about 180 US bombers were despatched against the oil installation at Ploesti, in Axis Rumania. They were picked up early by German radar and 54 were shot down; even Rumanian fighters shot some down.

The Allies were alert to the possibilities offered by the various Achilles heels of German industry. Oil was known to be a product which Germany could not easily obtain, and hence the raid on the oilfields. Another weak link was believed to be ball-bearing production, and for this reason it was decided to des-

These pages: One of the more versatile Luftwaffe aircraft. The Junkers Ju 88 was a ground-support aircraft, but the version shown here was in use as a night-fighter.

Above: The result of a raid on a German chemical plant. The blast effect of heavy bombs is evident and the hundreds of four-engined bombers which took part in such raids carried enough heavy bombs to ensure that at least two or three would drop just where they were needed. The power of their detonation did the rest.

Above right: A railroad tank-car has been thrown bodily off the track by bomb-blast. The Germans usually found that, when the site was cleared of wreckage, the damage was less than it had seemed.

troy the works at Schweinfurt. In one raid, 60 of the 376 Flying Fortresses were shot down, and in another 60 out of 291. At his point the Americans accepted that their bombers could not, after all, cope with German fighters. As for Schweinfurt, both the Americans and the Germans believed that a crippling blow had been struck, but in reality, not only was the damage soon repaired, but the Germans, to their surprise, discovered that slack accounting procedures meant that they had several month's supply of ball bearings in course of delivery or in store.

Luckily, the American dilemma had been foreseen. The conventional belief that a long-distance fighter, capable of escorting bombers over enemy territory, was not a good proposition because its long range would mean inferiority in other qualities, was shown to be false. At the beginning of 1944 the US daylight raids, suspended since the Schweinfurt setback, were ready to take off once more, thanks to the P-51 Mustang fighter. The Mustang was a highly successful combination of British engine and US airframe technology. Its engine was of Rolls-Royce design, but its body included improved American technologies. Not only that, but it had detachable fuel tanks that enabled it to fly deep into Germany where, having jettisoned its extra tanks, it had all the characteristics of a very advanced fighter.

This innovation not only enabled US day-

light bombers to get on with their job relatively untroubled by German fighters, but (more important, as some Americans though few others realized at the time) it was a means by which the Luftwaffe could be ground down until, by the time of the Normandy landings, it would be practically powerless. These bomber raids were a new form of attritional battle, with German fighter strength wasting away in daily combat against technically superior US fighters.

The Mustang, like almost all new designs, was really an improved version of old technology. When the war started in 1939 the metal piston-engined monoplane was almost at the end of its possibilities. Only by marginal improvements in armament, engines and other equipment was it possible to produce tactically superior models. Aircraft design and production were not handled intelligently either in Germany or Japan, probably because the nature of the ruling regimes did not encourage rational thought.

In Britain and the USA, despite occasional lapses, the right decisions were almost always made. One correct decision was to resist the temptation of introducing radically different designs. Aware that the design and development of new aircraft could take four or five years, the Allies concentrated on improving existing designs. The succession of improved Spitfires was perhaps an extreme example of this. This British fighter eventu-

ally was produced in 16 successive marks, or modifications, and was in production from the beginning to the end of the war. The Mark 1, which was so prominent in the Battle of Britain in 1940, consumed over 300,000 man-hours of design, but the total design man-hours spent on the 15 later versions only came to about 600,000. The economy of effort is clear, and was repeated in the factories where re-tooling for the new marks was far less disruptive than turning over to a completely new design. There were many other examples in US and British practice. Even the Mustang, so invaluable in 1944, was really an example of prewar technology, marginally improved, and with innovatory fuel tanks.

All in all, therefore, the aircraft used in the war by the British and Americans were essen-tially designs that already existed, at least on the drawing board, in 1940. Even the unusual British Mosquito, a highly successful fast bomber, was a blend of old technology, wooden construction, with the improved technology in piston-engine design.

In Germany the picture was very different and ultimately this was because neither the head of the Luftwaffe, Goering, nor Hitler, possessed the kind of mind that could under-stand the complexities of aircraft design and production. Both were addicted to the quick-fix, believing that new types could be de-signed, built and tested in a few months. The air force had considerable influence in the selection of types of development.

In Britain and the US, airmen, industrial managers, designers and officials would dis-

Above: Another view of B-17 bombers flying over England. With so many of the Superfortresses allocated to the Pacific war, the B-17 took the major share of bombing in the European theater.

cuss projects on a basis of equality. Such equality was lacking in Germany (even more so in Japan, where the social prestige of the officers meant that it was their views that prevailed). This was unfortunate for the Germans, because air force thinking was ill-informed and arrogant, and led to a chaotic situation in which far too many projects were selected for development, with far too few ever reaching production. Those that did reach an advanced stage usually failed to deliver the qualities that had been promised.

More fundamentally, the Nazi leaders were not proficient in long-term thinking.

Believing the war was almost over, and very satisfied with the performance of existing aircraft, the Nazi leadership in 1940 and 1941 imposed embargoes on development projects. Although these stoppages in due course were revoked, they delayed the development of new types by more than a year, and that was crucial. For example, airborne radar, essential for night-fighters, was among the projects delayed, which made Bomber Command's task easier up to 1944.

The Me 262, the first German jet-fighter, just like the first Allied jet, the British Meteor, had its roots in prewar research. But it was

delayed first by the embargo and then by Allied bombing, which meant that it was produced soon enough to go into successful service against US fighters over Germany, but late enough to ensure that there would be too few to affect the course of the war. It was only in 1944, when it was too late, that German project selection and development was reformed along more rational lines.

Probably strategic bombing cost the British more than it damaged the Germans up to about mid-1944, and the same may be true of the US bomber offensive in Europe. But in the end, after policies changed, the bomber did make a crucial difference. Acknowledgment that the bomber alone could not win the war came about the beginning of 1944, when the imminent Normandy landings forced the chiefs of staff and their political masters to review very seriously the role of air power.

The US Air Force could claim, with some photographic evidence, that it was damaging German industry, but German industry was still operating at full power, it seemed. RAF Bomber Command was unable to produce convincing evidence either that its efforts were paralyzing German industry or destroying German morale. Moreover, German radar-equipped night-fighters were making conventional night-bombing raids too costly. In a 795-bomber raid on Nurnberg in March, 94 aircraft were lost.

After the war it became clear that, despite the efforts of Allied bombers, efforts that had been largely directed at the German aircraft industry, German aircraft production nevertheless rose year by year. This was taken as proof that the bombing had been ineffective, although in reality the bombers did reduce the rate of German production from what it otherwise would have been.

All the same, the effectiveness of both American and British bombing increased enormously once the decision was made to aim not at indirect, but direct, support of the armies. In April Harris learned, to his dismay, that his fiefdom, Bomber Command, had been placed under Eisenhower, the supreme commander for the Normandy invasion. In the months before this transfer Bomber Command had been concentrating on Berlin, and Harris tried to persuade Churchill to invite the American bombers to join in, to "wreck Berlin from end to end" and thereby end the war.

In the meantime the US Eighth Air Force, stiffened with the new Mustang fighters, had renewed its assault on Germany. For some weeks bad weather had prevented much activity, but a clearing of the weather enabled

Main picture: US daylight bombing raids were an awesome spectacle. In this picture scores of B-17 Flying Fortresses fill the sky en route to a daylight raid on a small German industrial town. They are flying at about 24,000 feet, close to their optimum height with a 6000lb load. Although they were better armed than the Liberator, their range at not much more than 1000 miles was half that of the latter. The standard version carried 13 machine guns as well as three tons of bombs and could read speeds of about 300mph.

Above, far left: B-17s also attacked German-occupied Europe from bases in the Mediterranean theater. Here, a Flying Fortress comes to grief over its intended target, the railroad yards at Nis in Yugoslavia. It appears to have been hit or near-missed by anti-aircraft fire and is already disintegrating.

Above: Survivor of numerous bombing raids, as evidenced by its scoresheet below the cockpit, and with two of its officers awarded the Distinguished Flying Cross, an RAF Lancaster is toasted in the presence of its captain, crew, mascot and fitters.

the series of operations soon termed the "Big Week" to go forward in late February. In these days aircraft factories at Fürth, Stuttgart and Regensburg were attacked. Losses were quite small. For example on February 20 over 1000 bombers were sent against a dozen targets in Germany and only 21 were lost. Mustangs accounted for considerable numbers of German fighters both in the air and on the ground, for when the Mustangs faced no German fighters in the air they transferred their attention to ground targets.

In the weeks preceding D-Day both the US and British bombers, tactical as well as strategic, were given targets directly related to the coming battlefield in northern France. Transportation objectives had priority. In northern France, the Low Countries and western Germany the railroads became a prime object of attack. Harris was not happy with these targets, still believing that his pilots could not hit them. However, accuracy

had improved over the years, and in any case marshaling yards were big targets.

For the more precise targets like bridges, tunnels, junctions and locomotive depots the US strategic bombers had considerable success, especially as the Luftwaffe was unable to send more than a handful of fighters against them. Low-flying tactical bombers were also useful for destroying individual targets. The British Mosquito and the US Marauder twin-engined machines wreaked much destruction, and for raids on German airfields in France, were supplemented by fighter-bombers.

In early June efforts were shifted to softening up the German defenses in the invasion zone. However, the US 8th Air Force on June 2 sent almost 800 Flying Fortresses and Liberators to targets in the Calais area; this was to reinforce the impression that this was the area where the landings would be made. On D-Day, while Mustangs patrolled at the

higher altitudes to pounce on any German fighters that might appear, the 8th Air Force sent four waves of bombers to attack installations near the landing areas.

The first wave consisted of over 1350 heavy bombers, and of the four waves only three aircraft failed to return. At the same time the US 9th Air Force, using mainly twin-engined Marauders, was attacking coastal guns and transport centers from a lower level. Later, the strategic and tactical air forces supported the Avranches break-out of the US First Army. Then, while much of the strategic bomber strength was returned to targets in Germany, fighter-bombers continued to support the advancing Allied armies. Owing to lack of Luftwaffe opposition these activities were both destructive and cheap.

However, the Ardennes offensive launched by the Germans in December showed that despite their predominance in the air the Allies could not count on a con-

tinuous run of victories. In this "Battle of the Bulge," the Allied air forces were hampered, as Hitler had hoped, by bad weather, and it was only a few days of clear weather at the end of the month that enabled air power to make a significant contribution to the battle and turn the Germans back.

After the Allies had secured their position in Normandy, the bombers were concentrated against Germany itself, and in the last half of 1944, due to the absence of opposition, the improved accuracy, and the greater weight of aircraft employed, really substantial damage was done to the German economy. Apart from railroads, the German canal system suffered at the hands of Bomber Command. The US Air Force mounted another series of raids against oil installations. Lack of transport and lack of fuel at the end of 1944 meant that Germany could not make good use of the soldiers and material that still remained.

Above: The ball-bearing plant at Schweinfurt was regarded as an excellent target, because a few well-placed bombs could cripple many branches of war production. This is a picture of the second raid which took place in April 1944.

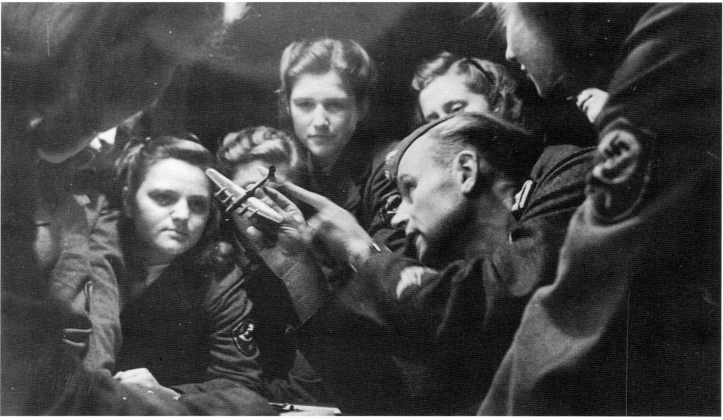

Before then, Hitler's last attempts at strategic bombing had come and gone. Never having had a true strategic bomber, Hitler was excited by the idea of the V-1 "flying bomb" and the V-2 rocket. Always susceptible to new technology, but rarely able to distinguish its genuinely useful features, he was entranced by these projects, which appeared to give him a new way of hitting back at the British bombing offensive. The first flying bomb fell on London in mid-June of 1944, causing a new evacuation of the British capital. These V-1s were more unnerving than the rockets which superseded them, because they could be seen by the naked eye and their drone could be heard until the engine cut off, leaving a long period of suspense during which people for miles around wondered where they would fall.

Coming in at any hour of night or day, they killed over 6000 Londoners. But by August most were being shot down, either by guns of by fighters. This was a useful role for the new Meteor jet fighters. Some of their launching sites had been bombed quite early after an alert French railroad official had noted the destination of the cement shipments needed for their launching pads, and had passed on his knowledge to the authorities in London via the French Resistance.

Most of the V-1 launching sites were soon overrun by the Allies in northern France, but the V-2 rockets were launched farther to the east. There was no defense against these; for the first time in its history Britain felt it was no longer an island. About 1100 V-2s were launched, killing 2750 people in southern England. In terms of damage inflicted against costs incurred, they were a remarkably inefficient weapon. In fact the British government, still not thoroughly grasping the irrationality of Nazi thought, believed the Germans would not continue to use them because they were so cost-ineffective.

When the scientists told Hitler that the V-2 would be inaccurate and would carry only a ton of warhead, less than the bombload of a conventional bomber, Hitler did not want to listen and insisted on allocating scarce resources to this weapon, confident that it would break British morale and thereby save him, at the last minute, from defeat. It did not turn out that way.

In 1940 Hitler had confounded both his own and enemy generals by doing what seemed irrational, and had won great successes. But that time was long past. He continued to do the irrational – his Ardennes offensive was an example – but the old tricks did not work any more.

Above left: A German V-1 is photographed as it falls on central London.

Left: Germans learn how to recognize and report enemy aircraft; a war publicity photograph of December 1944, one of several emphasizing the citizen's role in Germany's crisis.

Above: In the latter stages of the war interesting aircraft captured by the Allies were sent back for examination. This Me 110 with it striking radar array is being serviced by German ground crew before being sent to Britain.

CONCLUSION

Previous pages: A tank destroyer of the US 3rd Armored Division passes a knocked-out German Panzer IV in Belgium, January 1945.

In Britain and America and, naturally enough, France, the feeling at the end of 1944 was very different from that of the start of the year. Enough had happened to turn uncertainty into certainty.

The Russians called 1944 the "Year of the 10 Victories." Needless to say, those were all Russian victories. Although it was unfair to relegate the Battle of Normandy and other Allied successes to the category of also-rans, it can not be denied that it was in Russia that German armed power suffered the most wounding losses.

On the Western Front, the Allies would cross the Rhine in March 1945, and the German army, in which the teenage and elderly component was growing week by week, would offer only delaying tactics. The loss of

the Ruhr industrial area would guarantee that even if enough spirited troops could be found, material shortages would make any kind of counter-offensive a lost cause. The dwindling supplies of arms and ammunition would, in any case, be directed mainly to the Eastern Front.

Because so much of arms manufacturing had been dispersed, the Germans would find it possible, though difficult, in early 1945 to continue assembly of key items like aircraft. Despite heavy bombing, Germany had produced 36,000 new aircraft in 1944, about half what had been planned, but in 1945 not only territorial losses and continued bombing, but also Hitler's refusal to devote resources to the disgraced Luftwaffe, would mean that this production would tail off sharply.

The Luftwaffe, despite the difficulties, had managed to drop 9000 tons of bombs on Britain in 1944, but in 1945 would drop less than 800. No longer were Luftwaffe pilots highly trained; in 1944 new pilots spent less than half the hours in training that they had in 1939, which meant that they were receiving only a third of the training hours that new American and British pilots received.

Heavy bombing by the British and American air forces would continue until the very end of the war. To their joy, the British and US strategic bomber services had been released from their subordination to Eisenhower. Harris's Bomber Command had immediately returned to its old ways. It would again turn its attentions to Berlin but then, in February, would choose the ancient city of Dresden as the objective of a massive raid. Among the 25,000 dead were Allied prisoners of war and refugees, while Dresden, which had no military significance, was gutted. This bombing turned out to be a political error on Harris's part.

Hitherto the impression had been given that it was the Germans who specialized in terror bombing, and the 1940 burning of Coventry had been successfully portrayed as such, even though Coventry had been a major armaments center. The Dresden episode would encourage a new look at what Bomber Command had been doing. Harris

Main picture: General Patch's men cross the Rhine. The amphibious DUKW in which they are traveling, proved to be one of the most useful vehicles of World War II. The first bridge secured across the Rhine was at Remagen, captured in March 1945.

Above: By May 1945 the German Volkssturm, a kind of last-ditch home guard, was in action. This group is watching a demonstration of the "Panzerfaust" missile launcher.

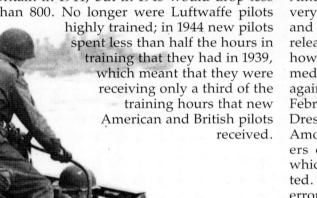

Above: The burnt-out Reichstag and general desolation in Berlin during late 1945. After the fall of the capital and death of Hitler, the German Reich survived for another week under Hitler's chosen successor, Admiral Dönitz.

would be virtually ostracized at the end of the war, and would not receive the expected postwar honors. He made an admirable scapegoat, and postwar critics of the bombing campaign would blame him rather than his political masters.

As for the US bombers, these too began again where they had left off. The 8th and 9th Air Forces in 1945 would continue their assaults on transportation and the oil industry, while the 12th and 15th would strike at central and southern Europe.

Finland had withdrawn from the war in 1944, freeing more Soviet troops for the drive into Germany. In January 1945 they would begin new offensives that would take them into eastern Germany and eventually Vienna, Prague and Berlin. A number of East Prussian villages captured in late 1944 had been treated as barbarously, if not more so, as some Russian villages had been treated by Germans, and the fate of Germans caught up in further Russian advances was a cause of great anxiety among German commanders. A well-known Soviet poet had written a poem for Soviet soldiers on the theme of "Kill! Kill!" and appeared to recommend, among other things, the rape of German women to break their racial pride. Disquieting facts and rumors were spreading in eastern Germany, and as the Russians advanced, refugees would pour westward.

In January the Allied plan for dividing Ger-

many into British, American and British zones had fallen into German hands. Admiral Dönitz, the U-boat specialist, who to his surprise became head of government after Hitler's demise in April, would be concerned above all to buy time in which the German population cut off by the Russian advance could be evacuated by sea. One of his first cares would be to dissuade the Nazi governor of Hamburg from making a separate peace with the Allies – Hamburg was essential for the sea evacuation. While still merely navy commander, Dönitz had concentrated the remains of his forces for this task and, between January and May, over two million people would be rescued, although there would be some spectacular tragedies when Soviet submarines succeeded in sinking crowded passenger liners.

Militarily, Dönitz would try, in his few days in office, to hold off the Western Allies as long as possible to save territory that was destined to become part of Western-occupied Germany; into this territory, he hoped, troops retreating from the Eastern Front could concentrate and then surrender to the British or Americans, thereby saving them from the grim fate that awaited those who fell into Russian hands.

To some degree Dönitz's policy would work, but the American commanders, more uncompromising than the British, would not listen to his appeals for more time and would

hand over many surrendered German troops to the oncoming Russians. Some of the lucky ones who were allowed to surrender in the west would not be so lucky after all, dying of starvation while in either British or American captivity.

France had gone from strength to strength and eventually, although this was not at first anticipated, she would have her own occupation zone in postwar Germany. For individual Frenchmen the reversals of fortune could be confusing, and many during the course of the war had fought on both sides. But any nation could find itself changing enemies. Britain, after all, had attacked the navy of its ally France in 1940, and in 1944 achieved another reversal when it despatched troops to suppress the anti-German Greek resistance.

The Germans had retreated from Greece and the local Resistance, which had played a large role in this, was triumphant. The Greek Resistance, however, was largely communist, so despite an uproar in the British press and a vote of censure in parliament, Churchill sent in troops to instal a safe provisional government.

Stalin raised no objections. He had already reached a gentleman's agreement with

Churchill about spheres of influence in postwar Europe, and he had observed scrupulously his part of the bargain. In Poland this mutual understanding would sour. The West wanted free elections but Stalin knew that free elections would deny him a pro-Russian government in Warsaw, so he would soon install his own puppet government. For thousands of Poles who had fought in the Allied forces this would mean that they would have no postwar home to go to. This was one of the several events that after the war would lead to what Hitler had so long been vainly counting on, a split between the Allies.

For Britain, this split would be no bad thing. Churchill had hoped that the war against Japan would last another 18 months, during which Britain would still receive US support but would gradually return to a peacetime economy. The swift termination of the Pacific war threatened an equally swift end to US assistance, and a rapid collapse of the British economy and British influence. But the elevation of Stalin's Russia to a new threat to world peace would alleviate the British dilemma. Churchill's last major service to his country would be his dramatization of the Soviet threat, bringing phrases like the "Cold War" and "Iron Curtain" into

Above: In mid-1945, after the American capture of Manila, General MacArthur inspects a prison that had been used for housing Allied prisoners. Western civilians had been sent to a concentration camp converted from a local university. Having a special personal interest in the Philippines, MacArthur spent a large proportion of his time on such visits.

American thoughts. This would achieve what the British government wanted, continuing status as an American ally.

The German and Japanese high commands, by the end of 1944, fully realized that defeat was inevitable, but could not bring themselves to admit it publicly. In both these countries, too, there were those who had no intention of surrendering. Some believed that the only respectable end was a fight to the last man, and suicide if necessary. Others put their hope in the emergence of a powerful secret weapon. This, of course, would materialize, at Hiroshima and Nagasaki, but for the Japanese it was the right weapon in the wrong hands at the wrong place.

In fact, with the failure of the V-2 rocket and the faltering production of jet aircraft, Germany had reached the end of its stock of new technology in 1944. Hitler, until his very end in April 1945, thought he might be saved by a split in the Allies' ranks. Roosevelt's death would excite him for that very reason, just two weeks before his own death by suicide.

The Japanese command at the end of 1944 still placed some hopes in its ability to surprise its enemies. But scientific research designed to create new war-winning technology did not flourish under Japan's militaristic rulers. They had little respect for academics, and their approach was to tell the scientists what they needed and then order them to do it. This was almost directly the reverse of what happened in Britain and the US, where scientists revealed what they thought might be possible and then, with government and military experts, decided which ideas should be pursued.

What made it worse for Japan was that the high command's idea of new weapons was limited to comic-strip concepts. Its most pressing demand, for example, was for a "death ray." By the end of the war the Japanese scientists would manage to produce a phenomenon which they called a "death ray." This could kill a rabbit at 1000 yards, but only if the rabbit consented to stand still for the five minutes needed for a lethal dose.

Much more important than new technology was new technique, and the US Navy was destined to suffer grievously in early 1945 from "Kamikaze" attacks. This technique, in which aircraft (and sometimes small boats) were crashed onto the chosen targets by their pilots, had appeared in 1944 but would be developed for the crucial final battles of the Pacific War. It would reach a peak in April 1945, with almost 1200 suicides, but then fell sharply away.

In the circumstances, it was a highly effective weapon, and certainly the best weapon the Japanese could use in 1945. A pool of trained or semi-trained pilots willing to end their lives in a blaze of patriotic glory was assured. The technique did not demand the latest types of aircraft, and in fact training aircraft and wood-and-fabric biplanes would appear on these missions.

Accuracy of aim was far greater than in conventional bombing for, even if a plane or its pilot was badly hit, momentum alone would often carry it to the target where escaping aviation fuel and the explosive

Below: In a lull during the hard-fought capture of Okinawa, Marines relax at Easter 1945. The Americans had landed on April 1, but it was not until June 21 that the last remnants of the 130,000 Japanese defenders of this 60-mile-long island were overcome.

Right: During the battle for Okinawa, a Marine patrol seeks to dislodge a Japanese sniper from a ruined church. The sniper is in the belfry, and while these two men cover his lair other Americans are approaching from the rear.

charge would constitute a deadly combination. About 400 Allied ships were hit, although only about 100 were badly damaged or sunk. The sinkings were of smaller ships, typically destroyers. The Australian cruiser *Australia* received four Kamikaze hits in four days off Luzon in January, but survived.

In the final development of the technique, attacks would no longer be individual but in waves, and US sailors had great difficulty in coping. Luckily, or wisely, since 1942 US ships and their crews had benefited from better firefighting installations and fire training. The latter had instilled in seamen the knowledge that even the most terrifying blaze could be quelled if approached calmly with the right equipment and the right procedure. Thanks to the New York City's fire department, a spray nozzle had been provided for fire hoses, and this was far more effective than simple water jets. Foam generators were provided for most fighting ships, as well as fire masks and helmets.

This mastery of firefighting probably saved many ships from destruction, although it did little to reduce the casualties from suicide planes. The latter would typically be aimed at the bridges or control centers of the target ships, and there were several cases of commanders and their staffs being burned to death. A late variant of the Kamikaze attacks would be piloted glider bombs, carried to the scene of action under specially adapted aircraft. These were more deadly, but the Japanese would not produce many of them.

Above: B-29 Superfortress bombers fly over Japanese territory as they continue their massive bombing campaign against military, urban, and industrial targets.

US carriers were particularly vulnerable because the suicide planes could penetrate several decks, starting dangerous fires and igniting aircraft. The four British fleet carriers taking part in the Okinawa operations benefited from their armored decks, and could be ready for action quite soon after a Kamikaze hit, and at this point in the campaign the armored deck, despite the weight disadvantage, seemed worthwhile – although the British carriers, because of this weight penalty, carried fewer planes and considerably less fuel than corresponding US carriers.

The British carriers and battleships would be off Okinawa largely at Churchill's urging, for he wanted Britain to be "in at the kill" of Japan. The US Navy, and some British staff officers, would have preferred the Royal Navy to have concentrated on the freeing of the Dutch East Indies, or Indonesia, in cooperation with the Australians and part of MacArthur's forces. But so long as the Japanese held Singapore this could hardly be done, and the British ships were transferred to the Pacific. One result of this would be that Allied forces did not approach the East Indies until a month after the Japanese surrender.

This gave time for local nationalists to gain power, and after a postwar year of struggle the Dutch government would decide that the East Indies were not worth fighting for. A similar situation, although longer delayed, would occur in French Indo-China and this, too, led to nationalists succeeding imperialists. Japan might have failed in its plan for an empire, but it did put an end to other Asian empires, although this would not become clear until later.

At the Quebec Conference in September 1944 the Allies had roughly sketched how the war with Japan would end. It was expected that this would occur 18 months after the end of the war in Europe, and would be preceded by landings in Japan itself. The southernmost island, Kyushu, would probably be invaded in October 1945 and the main island, Honshu, in January 1946. Russia would join in three months after the Germans surrendered, and could be expected to send troops into Japanese-held Manchuria. Heavy bombing of Japan from airfields in nearby islands would increase in intensity.

To secure airfields for the B-29 Superfortress bombers, and to bring the Allies within striking distance of the Japanese coast, several islands needed to be captured. At the

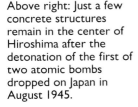

Above right: Just a few concrete structures remain in the center of Hiroshima after the detonation of the first of two atomic bombs dropped on Japan in August 1945.

start of 1945 the main island of the Philippines, Luzon, was at the top of the agenda, but attacks on Okinawa and Iwo Jima were also scheduled. Because the capture of Luzon was delayed by strong Japanese resistance, the assault on Iwo Jima would come only in February. This, too, would be bitterly defended, with the Japanese employing new tactics designed for the gradual attrition of the attackers' forces and a final stand in some corner of the island. At Iwo Jima the defenders would have time to build an intricate system of cave defenses and it would take a month to capture the island.

At Okinawa, even closer to Japan, the first landing would be on April 1. Contrary to expectations, the landings would not meet much resistance, but progress inland was desperately hard-fought. US shipping would have to face not only the Kamikazes but also the final throw of the Japanese navy, when the battleship *Yamato* emerged, carrying only enough fuel for the one-way trip to Okinawa. However, she would be sunk by air attack before she could take US ships under her guns.

It was not until July that Okinawa would be secured, but before then the final air assault would begin on the Japanese mainland. With convenient bases and little Japanese opposition, the B-29s would have little difficulty in burning city after city. On one day in March, 84,000 Japanese would be incinerated and 10-times that number made homeless. Japanese industry would also suffer badly, and by April Japan would have a new government headed by a former naval officer, a veteran of the Russo-Japanese War. Both he and his foreign minister and the emperor himself would realize that the war must be stopped, but with military diehards still in commanding positions this would not be easy. The population would be urged to prepare for a final struggle while, for reasons that remain controversial, the US government seemed unaware of Japanese peace feelers.

In early August Russia would join in, and the US atomic bomb dropped, but before then Japanese ministers would be quietly seeking peace. However, there would still be the powerful opposition of the old militarists with their prescription of a last-ditch, last-man defense of the national honor. Only the intervention of the emperor, and perhaps the thought that atomic bombs provided an honorable excuse, would overcome the resistance of that clique whose grotesque militarism had dominated Japan since the 1920s. Some of its members, even as the emperor was about to issue his proclamation on peace, would be vainly plotting to assassinate the prime minister and continue the war.

Index

Page numbers in *italics* refer to illustrations.

1944 – THE ALLIES TRIUMPH

Acknowledgments

The author and publisher would like to thank Mike Rose for designing this book, Suzanne O'Farrell for the picture research, Veronica Price and Nicki Giles for the production, Ron Watson for the index, and Richard Natkiel for the maps. The following provided photographic material:

Brompton Books Limited, pages: 11(top left and bottom), 14, 16(bottom), 34, 38(top left), 42, 46, 47(below right), 64, 65(top), 67(top), 87(left), 94(top) 100-101, 118(bottom), 145(below left), 168.
Bundesarchiv, pages: 16(top), 36, 37(top), 40(top), 67(bottom), 94(bottom), 100, 103, 105(bottom), 124-125, 126, 126-127, 144, 162(bottom), 167.
Hulton-Deutsch Collection, pages: 12, 45(bottom), 66, 68, 69, 70, 71, 80-81, 84(top), 88, 89(both), 118-119, 123, 125, 131(top), 136(top).
Imperial War Museum, London, pages: 1, 6-7, 9(both), 11(top right), 13(both), 23, 27(both), 29, 31(bottom), 33(inset), 37(bottom), 38(bottom), 40(bottom), 44(bottom), 45(top), 47(top and below left), 62-63, 75(both), 76, 76-77, 78(both), 79, 85, 86(both), 87(right), 90,
91(both), 95, 97(both), 98(bottom left and right), 101(bottom), 102(both), 104, 105(top), 112(top), 122-123, 131(bottom), 133(both), 134-135, 135, 137, 138(both), 140, 140-141, 142, 143, 146-147, 150, 150-151, 154-155, 158, 160, 161, 162(top), 163, 166-167.
Public Archives, Canada, pages: 8(NFB/C-21529), 44(top/DDD Army 38879).
UPI/Bettmann, pages: 170-171, 171.
U.S. Air Force, pages: 2-3, 15(bottom), 58(bottom), 60-61(top), 74, 148-149(all three), 152-153(all three), 156-157(all three), 158, 159, 172, 173.
U.S. Army, pages: 17, 26, 52-53, 53, 54-55, 55(top), 72-73, 84(bottom), 92-93, 109, 113, 128-129, 130, 132, 136(bottom), 143, 169.
U.S. Department of Defense, pages: 19(top), 20-21, 22-23, 48-49, 51(top), 54, 56, 57(both), 58(top), 59.
U.S. Marine Corps, page: 19(bottom).
U.S. National Archives, pages: 4-5, 7, 15(top), 18, 24-25, 28-29, 30, 31(top), 32-33, 38(top right), 38-39, 43(all three), 50, 51(bottom), 52, 60-61(bottom), 82(both), 83(both), 98-99, 106-107, 108(both), 110, 111, 114-115, 116, 116-117, 118-119, 118-119(inset), 139, 145(below right).
U.S. Naval Historical Center, pages: 112(bottom), 114(inset), 115(inset).
U.S. Signal Corps, pages: 41, 164-165.